New Jersey Parks, Forests, and Natural Areas

New Jersey Parks, Forests, and Natural Areas

A Guide

Third Edition

Michael P. Brown

RUTGERS UNIVERSITY PRESS

New Brunswick, New Jersey

Library of Congress Cataloging-in-Publication Data

Brown, Michael P., 1956–
    New Jersey parks, forests, and natural areas : a guide / Michael P. Brown.
      p.   cm.
    Includes bibliographical references and index.
    ISBN 0-8135-3399-6 (alk. paper)
    1. Outdoor recreation—New Jersey—Guidebooks. 2. Parks—New Jersey—
Guidebooks. 3. Natural areas—New Jersey—Guidebooks. 4. New Jersey—Guidebooks.
I. Title.
    GV191.42.N5B76   1997
    917.4904'43—dc21   97-17780
                                                                   CIP

A British Cataloging-in-Publication record for this book is available from the British Library.

Manufactured in the United States of America

√

To my mother, who helped instill in us
love for and excitement about nature.

Contents

REGION TWO   BERGEN, ESSEX, HUDSON, PASSAIC, & UNION COUNTIES

REGION THREE HUNTERDON, MERCER, MIDDLESEX, & SOMERSET COUNTIES 103

REGION FOUR   MONMOUTH & OCEAN COUNTIES   153

REGION FIVE   BURLINGTON, CAMDEN, GLOUCESTER, & SALEM COUNTIES   197

REGION SIX   ATLANTIC, CAPE MAY, & CUMBERLAND COUNTIES

New Jersey Parks, Forests, and Natural Areas

Introduction

New Jersey offers its residents a great variety of natural terrain with a wealth of landscapes. Forests, parks, recreation areas, and wildlife sanctuaries afford the visitor a chance to get away and enjoy the outdoors. Many have facilities for activities like swimming, boating, fishing, and hiking, while others provide a quiet place to see nature at its best.

This book includes national, state, county, and some municipal parks. I have also included some sites that are owned and managed by organizations, or even companies, but are open to the public for recreational use. In most instances, very small parks have been excluded unless they are especially significant in some way, or they pack an extraordinary amount of recreational possibilities into a small area. I have made an effort to visit a large number of the parks and to verify information from first-hand sources.

The emphasis of the book is on activities that the family can participate in together, such as swimming, boating, hiking, biking, and picnicking. Though most parks have a variety of sports facilities, they are not covered here. This information is available in park brochures and in other publications.

This edition has been thoroughly updated. Many parks have been added, and some have been deleted from the previous edition. I have striven to put added emphasis on handicap access at the parks. I have not included information on handicap parking, which is common in almost all parks.

I have also broadened coverage of mountain biking and horseback riding, two popular pastimes in many of our parks. I have attempted to include information on rock climbing also, but (contrary to what may be written on the internet or in other books) there are only a handful of parks in the state that allow this activity.

All telephone numbers have been updated, and I have included as many contact points within each park as possible. So, for instance, if you are interested in boating or fishing at a particular park, call the boathouse or bait shop first as an alternative to contacting the main office.

How to use this book

I have divided the state into six regions along county lines, and parks are listed alphabetically within each. A full-page map of each region shows the location of all parks mentioned. Areas that cover more than one county or region are listed under the one in which the majority of the area is located. If you are not sure of a park's location, check the index, which gives the page number of each park entry. I have chosen not to give specific directions to all of the parks; instead, I have supplied general locations. This will enable you, with the help of a good map, to find the path most appropriate for you.

Before you leave

CROWDS—For many of us, crowds are an unavoidable fact of life. As a general rule, most, if not all, areas are crowded on weekends and holidays, primarily during the spring and summer, though some are very crowded during the autumn color display. Consider visiting the parks during the off-season. Fewer services and facilities may be available (no swimming, fewer campsites, restricted office hours, etc.), but crowds and bothersome insects will be few, wildlife will be generally less inhibited, and the areas can be appreciated in new and exciting ways that may never have occurred to you.

FEES—Many of the national and state facilities charge an entrance fee. In most cases, the fee is in effect only from Memorial Day weekend to Labor Day. Areas charging a year-round fee often reduce it during the off-season. Though some areas have no entrance fee, spe-

Sayon Park.

cific activities such as boating or use of swimming beaches require a fee. If you plan on frequenting the state parks, consider acquiring a state park pass—for a flat fee it allows unlimited access. Call (800) 843-6420, or visit the New Jersey Division of Parks and Forestry website. A Golden Eagle Pass is also available for national parks, monuments, historic sites, recreation areas, and wildlife refuges that charge entrance fees. For more information, call (888) GO-PARKS [(888) 467-2757], or visit the National Park Service website at www. nationalparks.org.

In some instances a free county park can be a good substitute. This depends on the activities and services you are seeking. Many county parks offer excellent facilities and sites for a wide range of activities.

FISHING—Fishing is allowed, where available, only with a valid New Jersey fishing license. Licenses may be obtained at most sporting goods stores or bait and tackle shops. Children under fourteen are not required to have a license.

HUNTING—Many parks allow hunting in designated areas. These are generally far enough afield so that other visitors do not casually

Tripod Rock, Pyramid Mountain.

wander into the area. Nevertheless, if you think you will be in or near a hunting area, minimize danger by wearing blaze orange clothing. No hunting is allowed on Sunday, so this is a safe time to visit these locales. Hunting season is primarily from mid-October to late December. More exact information can be received from the Division of Fish, Game and Wildlife.

OUTDOOR ETIQUETTE—Trash and garbage strewn about is an eyesore to all who visit our parks. Follow the maxim of leave it as you wish you had found it, whether you are camping in a wilderness area or having a picnic. Most areas have receptacles for recycling—please use them. Plant and animal life should be left as undisturbed as possible, and bicycles, motor bikes, and horses shouldn't be used on trails unless specifically permitted.

Taking care of yourself

POISON IVY—It sometimes seems as if poison ivy is one of New Jersey's most vigorous plants. It is found in all parts of the state. It thrives along trails, roadsides, and other areas that have been disturbed. Avoid contact by learning to identify the plant. Even the bare vines in winter can cause irritation, and the smoke from burning poison ivy is especially dangerous.

BEES—Though bees, wasps, and yellow jackets usually don't sting if unprovoked, stings do occur. Avoid nests and swarms, and watch where you step if without shoes. Keep ointment in your first-aid box, which should always be with you on trips.

SNAKES—New Jersey has only two poisonous snakes, the copperhead and the timber rattler. A good rule to follow is: never put your hands anywhere you can't plainly see, such as inside rock crevices. Likewise, if you are walking barefoot, watch where you step.

SUNBURN—When outside, be particularly careful during the hottest part of the day, between 10:00 A.M. and 3:00 P.M. Wear a lightweight hat whenever possible, and apply sunscreen to exposed areas of skin.

LYME DISEASE—This is a tick-borne illness that can have potentially serious complications if left untreated. The disease is more common in the southern two-thirds of the state, but cases have been reported throughout the state. The best way to prevent the disease is to minimize contact with ticks. (The disease is transmitted by the deer tick, which is very small. The larger and more common wood tick is not a carrier.) Wear long pants, sneakers, or hard-soled shoes (not sandals), and tuck your pants into your socks. Ticks usually crawl around for several hours before attaching themselves to the skin, so careful inspection of skin and clothes as soon as you get home is very helpful.

Any flu-like symptoms, and often an expanding ring-like rash that occurs within two weeks should be seen by a doctor. More information can be obtained from state and county health offices and is frequently available in park offices as well.

RABIES—Though not common, rabies does exist in New Jersey. To minimize risk of infection, do not approach or handle wild animals— a rule that should be followed in any event.

ALTHOUGH I HAVE attempted to include the major parks in the state, I am well aware of how easy it is to miss places that deserve to be included. Suggestions and comments are welcome and will be incorporated whenever possible into later editions.

Region One

Sussex, Morris, & Warren Counties

Delaware Water Gap.

SUSSEX

MORRIS

12

15

23

40

42

7 LAYTON

36

2

VERNON

41

39

206

94

13

37

28

NEWTON

34

45

18

15

43

BLAIRSTOWN

47

44

21

33

6

94

HOPATCONG

31

30

5

519

46

80

17

287

1

16

3

38

HACKETTSTOWN

35

14

80

29

206

4

MORRISTOWN

25

26

OXFORD

32

8

22

31

CHESTER

24

19

20

24

11

23

9

10

27

WARREN

Parks

• Selected Towns

Selected Roads

County Borders

-N-

0   5
miles

1   Allamuchy Mountain State Park
2   Bear Swamp Wildlife Management Area
3   Berkshire Valley Wildlife Management Area
4   Black River Wildlife Management Area
5   Columbia Lake Wildlife Management Area
6   Delaware Water Gap National Recreation Area
7   Flatbrook-Roy Wildlife Management Area
8   Frelinghuysen Arboretum
9   Great Swamp National Wildlife Refuge
10 Great Swamp Outdoor Education Center
11 Hacklebarney State Park
12 Hainesville Wildlife Management Area
13 Hamburg Mountain Wildlife Management Area
14 Hedden Park
15 High Point State Park
16 Hopatcong State Park
17 Jenny Jump State Forest
18 Kittatinny Valley State Park
19 Lewis Morris Park
20 Loantaka Brook Reservation
21 Mahlon Dickerson Reservation
22 Merrill Creek Reservoir Environmental Preserve
23 Morristown National Historic Park
24 Musconetcong River Wildlife Management Area
25 Old Troy Park
26 Oxford Furnace Lake Park
27 Passaic River Park
28 Paulinskill River Wildlife Management Area
29 Pequest Wildlife Management Area
30 Pyramid Mountain Natural Historical Area
31 Rockaway River Wildlife Management Area
32 Schooley's Mountain Park
33 Silas Condict Park
34 Sparta Mountain Wildlife Management Area
35 Stephens State Park
36 Stokes State Forest
37 Swartswood State Park
38 Tourne Park
39 Trout Brook Wildlife Management Area
40 Wallkill River National Wildlife Refuge
41 Walpack Wildlife Management Area
42 Wawayanda State Park
43 Weldon Brook Wildlife Management Area
44 White Lake Wildlife Management Area
45 Whittingham Wildlife Management Area
46 Wildcat Ridge Wildlife Management Area
47 Worthington State Forest

Allamuchy Mountain State Park

Hackettstown, Sussex, and Warren Counties ◆
7,646 acres

LOCATION: The park is located 3 miles north of Hackettstown, between Willow Grove/Waterloo Road (Route 604) on the east, Route 517 on the west, and Cranberry Lake (Route 206) on the north.

HOURS: Dawn to dusk.

ENTRANCE FEE: None.

HANDICAP ACCESS: Only the boat launch area at Cranberry Lake is handicap accessible.

SPECIAL FEATURES

Waterloo Village—A restored nineteenth-century Morris Canal port town. Open to visitors from mid-April through December. For more information, call (973) 347-0900, or visit www.waterloo-village.org.

BOATING: Allowed in 179-acre Cranberry Lake. A trailer and car-top boat launch is available for public use.

FISHING: Permitted in 50-acre Allamuchy Pond, in 46-acre Deer Park Pond, and in Cranberry Lake, for largemouth bass, sunfish, catfish, pickerel, and perch.

HIKING: There are four marked trails, totaling fifteen miles, and twenty-five miles of unmarked trails.

MOUNTAIN BIKING: Permitted on all trails.

HORSEBACK RIDING: Permitted on all trails.

HUNTING: Permitted in designated areas of the park (5,023 acres), for deer, small game, turkey, and waterfowl.

WINTER ACTIVITIES: Cross-country skiing, snowshoeing, and ice fishing.

For additional information:
c/o Stephens State Park
800 Willow Grove Street
Hackettstown, NJ 07840
Telephone: (908) 852-3790

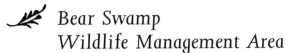

Bear Swamp
Wildlife Management Area

Sussex County ◆ *2,036 acres*

LOCATION: West of Route 206, and east of Route 521, in the vicinity of Culvers Inlet.

HOURS: Dawn to dusk.

ENTRANCE FEE: None.

HANDICAP ACCESS: None.

HIKING: Informal trails.

MOUNTAIN BIKING: Allowed on existing trails and secondary roads from March 1 to April 15, and from June 1 to September 15, as well as on all Sundays throughout the year.

HUNTING: For deer, small game, and turkey.

WINTER ACTIVITIES: Cross-country skiing on all trails on Sunday.

For additional information:
New Jersey Division of Fish and Wildlife
Trenton Office
501 E. State Street, P.O. Box 400
Trenton, NJ 08625–0400
Telephone: (609) 984-0547

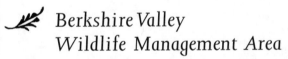

Berkshire Valley
Wildlife Management Area

Morris County ◆ *1,848 acres*

LOCATION: South of the town of Mt. Arlington. Access is from the Union Turnpike (Route 15). Off-the-road parking is permitted in most areas.

HOURS: Dawn to dusk.

ENTRANCE FEE: None.

HANDICAP ACCESS: None.

FISHING: Permitted in the Rockaway River, which is stocked with trout.

HIKING: Informal trails.

MOUNTAIN BIKING: Allowed on existing trails and secondary roads from March 1 to April 15, and from June 1 to September 15, as well as on all Sundays throughout the year.

HUNTING: For deer, small game, turkey, and waterfowl.

WINTER ACTIVITIES: Cross-country skiing on all trails on Sunday.

For additional information:
New Jersey Division of Fish and Wildlife
Trenton Office
501 E. State Street, P.O. Box 400
Trenton, NJ 08625–0400
Telephone: (609) 984-0547

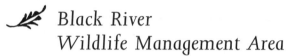

Black River
Wildlife Management Area

Morris County ◆ *3,042 acres*

LOCATION: Access to the tract is from North Road (Route 513), and Pleasant Hill Road, both approximately 2 miles northeast of Chester. North Road leads to the office.

Michael Brown

Black River.

HOURS: Dawn to dusk.

ENTRANCE FEE: None.

HANDICAP ACCESS: None.

FISHING: Permitted in the Black River.

HIKING: Informal trails.

MOUNTAIN BIKING: Allowed on existing trails and secondary roads from March 1 to April 15, and from June 1 to September 15, as well as on all Sundays throughout the year.

HORSEBACK RIDING: Allowed on all trails, with a permit.

HUNTING: For deer, small game, turkey, and waterfowl.

WINTER ACTIVITIES: Cross-country skiing on all trails on Sunday.

For additional information:
New Jersey Division of Fish and Wildlife
Trenton Office
501 E. State Street, P.O. Box 400
Trenton, NJ 08625–0400
Telephone: (609) 984-0547

 # Columbia Lake
Wildlife Management Area

Warren County ◆ *654 acres*

LOCATION: North and south of I–80, and east of Routes 34 and 46. Access is from a dirt road off Route 46, in the town of Columbia, or from Warrington-Polkville Road, off Route 94.

HOURS: Dawn to dusk.

ENTRANCE FEE: None.

HANDICAP ACCESS: None.

BOATING: Allowed on 55-acre Columbia Lake, with car-top boat launch.

FISHING: Good fishing for a large variety of fish. A large shoreline is available for bank fishing.

HIKING: Informal trails.

MOUNTAIN BIKING: Allowed on existing trails and secondary roads from March 1 to April 15, and from June 1 to September 15, as well as on all Sundays throughout the year.

HUNTING: For deer, small game, and waterfowl.

WINTER ACTIVITIES: Cross-country skiing on all trails on Sunday.

> **For additional information:**
> *New Jersey Division of Fish and Wildlife*
> *Trenton Office*
> *501 E. State Street, P.O. Box 400*
> *Trenton, NJ 08625–0400*
> *Telephone: (609) 984-0547*

 # Delaware Water Gap National Recreation Area

Sussex and Warren Counties • *70,000 acres*

LOCATION: Kittatinny Point Visitor Center is located on the Delaware River, just off I–80, at New Jersey exit 1, westbound. (Eastbound, take the first ramp after the toll plaza.) Bushkill Visitor Center is located one-tenth of a mile south of the blinking light on Route 209, in Bushkill, Pa., in the former St. John's church.

HOURS: The grounds are open from dawn to dusk. Kittatinny Point Visitor Center is open daily during the summer, from 9:00 A.M. to 5:00 P.M.; call for winter hours. Bushkill Visitor Center is open daily during the summer, from 9:00 A.M. to 5:00 P.M.; call for winter hours. Park Headquarters is open weekdays, except on federal holidays, from 8:00 A.M. to 4:30 P.M.

ENTRANCE FEE: In New Jersey, fees are collected at Depew and Watergate Recreation sites. In Pennsylvania, fees are collected at Milford Beach, Dingmans Ferry Access, Bushkill Access, and Smithfield Beach.

HANDICAP ACCESS: The five-mile Joseph M. McDade Recreational Trail is wheelchair accessible. The picnic area at Milford Beach is accessible, as is the half-mile- long boardwalk trail at Dingmans Falls. For additional information on other park sites that are handicap accessible, call (570) 588-2452.

DESCRIPTION: Created in 1965, the park includes land in both Pennsylvania and New Jersey, stretching thirty-seven miles along the Delaware River (designated a wild and scenic river). The park includes a wide variety of terrain, from heavily forested mountains to farmland, and is named after the Delaware Water Gap—a mile-wide gorge cut by the river through the Kittatinny Mountains.

SPECIAL FEATURES

Millbrook Village—Re-creation of a late-nineteenth-century rural community. The village is staffed on Saturdays and Sundays, from May through October. For additional information, call (908) 841-9531.

Pocono Environmental Educational Center—Educational displays, information, gift shop, and restrooms. For more information, call (570) 828-2319, or visit www.peec.org.

Bushkill Visitor Center—Exhibits, information, and trail maps. This center is located in Bushkill, Pa. For more information, call (570) 588-7044.

Kittatinny Visitor Center—Exhibits, information, and trail maps. Portable toilets (handicap accessible) are available when the Visitor Center is closed. Located in Columbia, N.J. For more information, call (908) 496-4458.

PICNICKING: Can be enjoyed at various sites. Popular spots on the New Jersey side are at Watergate and Millbrook.

BOATING: The Delaware River is generally considered an easy river for canoeing. Public boat launches can be found every eight to ten miles, and private boat liveries in the area provide boat rentals, additional launching sites, and boat pickup. Boat launches are also located at Kittatinny Visitor Center, Milford Beach, and Smithfield Beach.

FISHING: Permitted in the lakes and streams of the park, as well as in the Delaware River. Flatbrook Creek is stocked with trout. Pickerel, sunfish, and rock bass are generally found in the lakes and ponds. The Delaware River contains carp, catfish, shad, smallmouth bass, and walleye.

SWIMMING: Lifeguard-supervised swimming is available at Milford Beach and Smithfield Beach, both on the Pennsylvania side. On the New Jersey side, lifeguard-supervised swimming is available at Depew Recreation site. (Portable toilets only.)

HIKING: Six marked trails of varying length and difficulty begin and end at the Pocono Environmental Education Center. Numerous other trails (comprising more than sixty miles) are found throughout the park, including a twenty-five-mile portion of the Appalachian Trail.

HORSEBACK RIDING: Upper Ridge Trail near Layton, New Jersey, offers five miles of trails for horseback riding. For additional information, call (570) 588-2451.

ROCK CLIMBING: Permitted in the park. A climbing guide is sold at visitor centers.

HUNTING: Permitted in specific areas of the park.

WINTER ACTIVITIES: Cross-country skiing can be enjoyed on many of the trails in the park. Ice fishing is also permitted.

> **For additional information:**
> Bushkill, PA 18324–9999
> Telephone: (570) 588-2452; Fax: (570) 588-2780;
> Website: www.nps.gov/dewa

Flatbrook-Roy
Wildlife Management Area

Sussex County • 2,090 acres

LOCATION: Adjacent to Stokes State Forest, and south of the town of Layton. From Route 206, turn west onto Route 521, then turn onto Route 615, which runs through the tract.

HOURS: Dawn to dusk.

ENTRANCE FEE: None.

HANDICAP ACCESS: A crushed-stone area along a retaining wall, located in the fly-fishing section, is handicap accessible.

FISHING: Good fishing on the Big Flat Brook and on Little Flat Brook, two well-known trout streams. Trout are stocked at regular intervals.

HIKING: Informal trails.

MOUNTAIN BIKING: Allowed on existing trails and secondary roads from March 1 to April 15, and from June 1 to September 15, as well as on all Sundays throughout the year.

HORSEBACK RIDING: Allowed on all trails, with a permit.

HUNTING: For deer, small game, turkey, and waterfowl.

WINTER ACTIVITIES: Cross-country skiing on all trails on Sunday.

For additional information:
New Jersey Division of Fish and Wildlife
Trenton Office
501 E. State Street, P.O. Box 400
Trenton, NJ 08625–0400
Telephone: (609) 984-0547

Frelinghuysen Arboretum

53 East Hanover Avenue ◆ Hanover and Morris Townships ◆ Morris County ◆ 127 acres

LOCATION: From I–287, exit to Morris Avenue, and go east to Whippany Road. Continue to the second traffic light, then turn west onto East Hanover Avenue. Continue for approximately 0.25 miles. The entrance to the arboretum is opposite the Morris County Library.

HOURS: The grounds are open from dawn to dusk. The Education Center is open Monday through Saturday, from 9:00 A.M. to 4:30 P.M., and on Sunday, from 12:00 P.M. to 4:30 P.M.

Morris County Park Commission

Frelinghuysen Arboretum.

ENTRANCE FEE: None.

HANDICAP ACCESS: There is a Braille trail for the visually impaired.

DESCRIPTION: Serves as the headquarters of the Morris County Park Commission, which is housed in the Frelinghuysen Mansion. This is an official historic site, and the first floor of the building is open to the public. There are extensive gardens, including large lilac and rose collections. The Education Center has a library that is open to the public and that serves as a nexus for services to the gardening public.

SPECIAL FEATURES

Arboretum—Formal gardens and a collection of plants suited to the soils and climate of Morris County.

Joseph F. Haggerty Education Center—Features exhibits and information. The focus of the center is to provide horticultural education to the public.

HIKING: There are two self-guided trails, plus part of the Patriots' Path.

For additional information:
Morris County Park Commission
53 East Hanover Avenue
P.O. Box 1295
Morristown, NJ 07962–1295
Telephone: (973) 326-7600; Fax: (973) 644-2726

ꙮ Great Swamp National Wildlife Refuge

Morris County ♦ 7,500 acres

LOCATION: From I–287, exit to North Maple Avenue, Basking Ridge. Go 1.5 miles to the first traffic light, and turn east onto Madisonville Road. Continue on for 2.7 miles, and turn south onto Long Hill Road. Proceed 2.2 miles to the entrance of the Wildlife Observation Center, on the north side of the road. To arrive at the refuge headquarters, continue on Long Hill Road. Turn west onto White Bridge Road, and north again onto Pleasant Plains Road.

HOURS: Dawn to dusk.

ENTRANCE FEE: None.

Boardwalk at Great Swamp.

HANDICAP ACCESS: The refuge office and the trails at the Wilderness Observation Center are handicap accessible.

DESCRIPTION: Established in 1960, the refuge provides a unique wilderness area in close proximity to densely populated northern New Jersey. It consists of swamp woodlands, meandering brooks, hardwood forests, marshes, and grasslands.

SPECIAL FEATURES

Wildlife Observation Center—The center has extensive information about park flora and fauna, boardwalk trails, blinds for observing wildlife, and modern restroom facilities. For more information, call (973) 425-1222.

HIKING: Nine miles of walking trails and boardwalks.

BIRDWATCHING: Blinds for observing birds are located at several locations throughout the park.

HUNTING: For deer.

WINTER ACTIVITIES: Cross-country skiing.

For additional information:
152 Pleasant Plains Road
Basking Ridge, NJ 07920–9615
Telephone: (973) 425-1222; *Fax:* (973) 425-7309;
Website: www.greatswamp.fws.gov

 # Great Swamp Outdoor Education Center

247 Southern Boulevard ♦ Chatham, Morris County ♦
60 acres

LOCATION: Take Route 24 to Fairmount Avenue, and then to Southern Boulevard, heading north. The Education Center is on the west side of the road.

HOURS: The grounds are open from dawn to dusk. The Education Center is open seven days a week (except holidays), from 9:00 A.M. to 4:30 P.M.

ENTRANCE FEE: None.

HANDICAP ACCESS: A half-mile boardwalk trail is wheelchair accessible, and the Education Center is handicap accessible.

SPECIAL FEATURES

The Education Center—Displays, dinosaur footprints, a library, an auditorium, and restrooms. For more information, call (973) 635-6629.

HIKING: Five marked or self-guided trails, many on boardwalks through the swamp. A trail map and brochure are available.

BIRDWATCHING: An observation blind is located near the pond, a short walk from the parking area.

For additional information:
Morris County Park Commission
P.O. Box 1295
Morristown, NJ 07962–1295
Telephone: (973) 326-7600; *Fax:* (973) 644-2726;
Website: www.parks.morris.nj.us

 # Hacklebarney State Park

Chester, Morris County ♦ 977 acres

LOCATION: Entrance to the park is on Hacklebarney State Park Road, north of Route 512, and west of Route 206.

HOURS: Dawn to dusk.

ENTRANCE FEE: None.

HANDICAP ACCESS: None.

DESCRIPTION: Considered one of the most picturesque parks in the state, both for the beautiful setting of the Black River gorge, and for the brilliant autumn color display.

PICNICKING: There are several sites throughout the park, with grills and restrooms.

FISHING: Permitted in the Black River, which is stocked annually with trout.

HIKING: Marked and unmarked trails.

HUNTING: Permitted in designated areas of the park (628 acres), for deer, small game, and turkey.

WINTER ACTIVITIES: Cross-country skiing.

> **For additional information:**
> *c/o Voorhees State Park*
> *119 Hacklebarney Road*
> *Long Valley, NJ 07853–9525*
> *Telephone: (908) 638-6969*

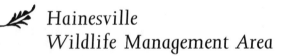

Hainesville Wildlife Management Area

Sussex County • *282 acres*

LOCATION: Adjacent to High Point State Park, northeast of Hainesville. From Route 206, turn east onto Shaytown Road. Then turn north onto New Road, which passes through the tract and provides access to the lake.

HOURS: Dawn to dusk.

ENTRANCE FEE: None.

HANDICAP ACCESS: None.

BOATING: Car-top boat launch.

FISHING: Permitted in the 30-acre pond and in the Little Flat Brook.

HIKING: Informal trails.

MOUNTAIN BIKING: Allowed on existing trails and secondary roads from March 1 to April 15, and from June 1 to September 15, as well as on all Sundays throughout the year.

HUNTING: For deer, small game, turkey, and waterfowl.

WINTER ACTIVITIES: Cross-country skiing on all trails on Sunday.

> **For additional information:**
> New Jersey Division of Fish and Wildlife
> Trenton Office
> 501 E. State Street, P.O. Box 400
> Trenton, NJ 08625—0400
> Telephone: (609) 984-0547

🌿 Hamburg Mountain Wildlife Management Area

Sussex County • *2,736 acres*

LOCATION: Approximately 2 miles east of Franklin, off Routes 517 and 23. Adjacent to the Vernon Valley/Great Gorge Ski Resort.

HOURS: Dawn to dusk.

ENTRANCE FEE: None.

HANDICAP ACCESS: None.

BOATING: Car-top boat launch.

FISHING: Permitted in Gorge Lake and in Stewart Lake. Franklin Pond Creek, which flows along Route 23 on the southern border of the tract, is stocked with trout.

HIKING: Informal trails.

MOUNTAIN BIKING: Allowed on existing trails and secondary roads from March 1 to April 15, and from June 1 to September 15, as well as on all Sundays throughout the year.

HUNTING: For deer, small game, turkey, and waterfowl.

WINTER ACTIVITIES: Cross-country skiing on all trails on Sunday.

> **For additional information:**
> New Jersey Division of Fish and Wildlife
> Trenton Office
> 501 E. State Street, P.O. Box 400
> Trenton, NJ 08625—0400
> Telephone: (609) 984-0547

Hedden Park

124 Reservoir Avenue and Concord Road ◆
Dover, Mine Hill, and Randolph Townships ◆
Morris County ◆ *380 acres*

LOCATION: From Route 10, southwest of Dover, take Route 513 north to Reservoir Avenue. Turn west onto Randolph Avenue from Route 513, and enter from Concord Road.

HOURS: Dawn to dusk.

ENTRANCE FEE: None.

HANDICAP ACCESS: A fishing pier is handicap accessible.

PICNICKING: Tables with grills, a playground, and a restroom.

BOATING: Allowed on the 6-acre lake. Boat rentals are available at the boathouse, which is open from Memorial Day weekend to Labor Day, on Saturday and Sunday, from 11:00 A.M. to 5:30 P.M. For more information, call (973) 361-9848.

FISHING: Permitted in the lake.

HIKING: Five marked trails.

WINTER ACTIVITIES: Cross-country skiing and ice skating.

For additional information:
Morris County Park Commission
53 East Hanover Avenue, P.O. Box 1295
Morristown, NJ 07962–1295
Telephone: (973) 326-7600; Fax: (973) 644-2726

High Point State Park

Sussex County ◆ *15,149 acres*

LOCATION: The park office is on Route 23, 8 miles northwest of Sussex.

HOURS: The grounds are open from dawn to dusk. The park office is open from Memorial Day weekend to Labor Day, Sunday through Thursday, from 8:00 A.M. to 4:00 P.M., and on Friday and Saturday, from 8:00 A.M. to 8:00 P.M. During the winter, the office is open daily, from 8:00 A.M. to 4:00 P.M. The park Interpretive Center has similar hours.

ENTRANCE FEE: A fee is charged from Memorial Day weekend to Labor Day.

High Point State Park.

HANDICAP ACCESS: The majority of buildings at the park are handicap accessible. Call the office for details.

DESCRIPTION: Located along the crest of the Kittatinny Mountains, at the highest point in New Jersey (1,803-foot elevation).

SPECIAL FEATURES

High Point Monument—Located north of Lake Marcia, on Monument Drive. The 220-foot monument is dedicated to the memory of New Jersey's wartime heroes.

Cross-country Ski Center—Information and refreshments. For more information, call (973) 702-1222 (from December 1 to March 31).

The Interpretive Center—Displays, exhibits, information, and maps of the park. Restrooms are also available.

CABINS: Two cabins, each accommodating six people, are located along the shore of Steenykill Lake. Cabins have full kitchens and bathrooms, and electricity. Wood stoves provide heat. They are open from May 15 to October 15. Reservations are required.

CAMPING: Fifty sites for tent camping are situated along 20-acre Sawmill Lake. Each site has a picnic table and fire ring. Flush toilets and drinking water are available. The camping season is from April 1 to October 31.

PICNICKING: Several picnic areas are located between the park office and Lake Marcia. Tables and grills, or fireplaces, are provided.

BOATING: Car-top boat launches are located at 20-acre Sawmill Lake, and at 30-acre Lake Steenykill. Powered boats are limited to electric motors.

SWIMMING: A lifeguard-supervised bathing beach is located at 20-acre Lake Marcia. The lake is spring fed, and the water is cool. Restrooms, changing rooms, a food concession (during the summer), and playground equipment are nearby.

FISHING: Permitted in the lakes and streams of the park.

HIKING: Nine marked trails, in addition to a large segment of the Appalachian Trail.

MOUNTAIN BIKING: Permitted on specific trails.

HORSEBACK RIDING: Permitted on specific trails.

HUNTING: Permitted in designated areas of the park (3,089 acres), for deer, small game, turkey, and waterfowl. Deer hunting is allowed on 8,000 acres, by special permit only.

WINTER ACTIVITIES: Cross-country skiing (on thirteen miles of trails), snowmobiling (on twenty miles of trails and other routes).

For additional information:
1480 State Road 23
Sussex, NJ 07461
Telephone: (973) 875-4800; Fax: (973) 875-8084

 Hopatcong State Park

Landing, Morris County • 107 acres

LOCATION: North of exit 28, off of I–280, at the southwestern end of Lake Hopatcong.

HOURS: The grounds are open Memorial Day weekend to Labor Day, from 8:00 A.M. to 8:00 P.M.; otherwise, they are open from dawn to dusk. From the day after Labor Day until the day before Memorial Day, boat launching is permitted.

ENTRANCE FEE: There is a fee charged from Memorial Day weekend to Labor Day.

HANDICAP ACCESS: A floating dock is wheelchair accessible, as well as the shoreline.

DESCRIPTION: This park includes a section of the old Morris Canal from 1832.

SPECIAL FEATURES

Lake Hopatcong Historical Museum—Located in a nineteenth-century lock tender's house, the museum traces the history of the lake and its surrounding area. Call for opening times: (973) 398-2616.

PICNICKING: On a wooded slope near the beach, with playgrounds.

BOATING: A boat ramp is located next to the swimming area. No boat rentals are available. There are no restrictions on types of boats.

SWIMMING: A well-graded lawn, sloping toward the lake, is available for those using the lake. The beach is supervised during the summer. A bathhouse and concession stand are open from May through Labor Day.

FISHING: Permitted in 2,685-acre Lake Hopatcong, which is stocked with trout each spring. Other species include bass, pickerel, perch, and catfish.

WINTER ACTIVITIES: Ice fishing, ice skating, ice boating, sledding, and ice sailing.

For additional information:
P.O. Box 8519
Landing, NJ 07850–8519
Telephone: (973) 398-7010

 Jenny Jump State Forest

Hope, Warren County • 3,985 *acres*

LOCATION: The park office is located on State Park Road, 3 miles south of County Road 519.

HOURS: The grounds are open from dawn to dusk; the office is open daily, from 8:30 A.M. to 4:00 P.M.

ENTRANCE FEE: None.

Jenny Jump State Forest.

Michael Brown

HANDICAP ACCESS: Two camp shelters are partially handicap accessible. There is handicap accessibility to fishing at Ghost Lake.

SPECIAL FEATURES

    Greenwood Observatory—The United Astronomy Clubs of New Jersey (UACNJ) leases property from the New Jersey Department of Environmental Protection and runs the observatory. Public programs are held on Saturday, April through October, from 8:00 A.M. to10:00 P.M. For additional information, refer to their website: www.uacnj.org.

SHELTERS: Eight shelters are located near the top of Jenny Jump Mountain. Each has two bunk rooms with two double-deck beds, a small living room with a wood-burning stove for heat, and a screened door and windows. Modern restroom facilities and showers are located near the picnic area, a relatively short walk from the shelters. The shelters are open year-round and can be reserved for two to fourteen nights.

CAMPING: Twenty-two wooded sites (primarily for tents) are provided. Some are walk-in sites only. Each site has a fire ring and table. Drinking water is available, and toilets, showers, and a small playground are nearby. The camping area is open from April 1 through October 31.

PICNICKING: A large, wooded picnic area with grills is located near the top of Jenny Jump Mountain, close to the entrance for the park. A small playground and modern restroom facilities are nearby.

BOATING: Canoeing is allowed in 2-acre Ghost Lake. Parking for the lake is on Shades of Death Road.

FISHING: Permitted in Ghost Lake, for bass, crappie, sunfish, and catfish.

HIKING: Six marked trails, ranging from 0.3 miles to 3.7 miles.

MOUNTAIN BIKING: The Mountain Lake trail is 3.7 miles, and is also open for mountain biking.

HUNTING: Permitted in designated areas of the park (2,193 acres), for deer, small game, turkey, and waterfowl.

WINTER ACTIVITIES: Cross-country skiing.

For additional information:
P.O. Box 150
Hope, NJ 07844
Telephone: (908) 459-4366

 Kittatinny Valley State Park

Andover, Sussex County ♦ *3,350 acres*

LOCATION: From Route 80, take Route 206 north approximately 7 miles to Andover Borough. Turn right onto County Route 669 (Limecrest Road). The park entrance is 1.1 miles ahead, on the left.

HOURS: The grounds are open from dawn to dusk; the park office is open daily, from 8:00 A.M. to 4:30 P.M., dependent upon staffing.

ENTRANCE FEE: None.

HANDICAP ACCESS: Restrooms are handicap accessible, and the fishing pier at Lake Aeroflex provides handicap access to the lake.

PICNICKING: Tables with grills, and a restroom nearby.

BOATING: Allowed in 117-acre Lake Aeroflex (with ramp for trailer and car-top), in 39-acre Gardner's Pond (walk-in access), in Twin Lakes (with car-top access), and in Whites Pond (walk-in access). Electric motors only.

FISHING: Excellent fishing in both the lakes and the ponds.

HIKING: Informal trails.

MOUNTAIN BIKING: Permitted on all trails.

HORSEBACK RIDING: Permitted on all trails.

HUNTING: Permitted in designated areas (1,148 acres), for deer, small game, turkey, and waterfowl.

WINTER ACTIVITIES: Cross-country skiing.

For additional information:
P.O. Box 621
Andover, NJ 07821–0621
Telephone: (973) 786-6445

Lewis Morris Park

270 Mendham Road ◆ Harding, Mendham, and Morris Townships ◆ Morris County ◆ 1,154 acres

LOCATION: Access is via the Jockey Hollow section of Morristown National Historic Park (from Sugar Loaf Road), or from Route 24, approximately 3 miles west of Morristown. There are two

Lewis Morris Park.

entrances on Route 24. The eastern entrance leads to the lake and picnic sites.

HOURS: The grounds are open from dawn to dusk. The bath/boathouse is open from late June until Labor Day, Wednesday through Friday, from 11:00 A.M. to 5:30 P.M., and on weekends, from 11:00 A.M. to 6:30 P.M. Open weekends only from Memorial Day until late June.

ENTRANCE FEE: A fee is charged for use of the swimming area from Memorial Day weekend to Labor Day.

HANDICAP ACCESS: A handicap-accessible ramp has been added to the beach and to the snack bar entrance. There is also access to the boating area and restrooms.

PICNICKING: Tables with grills, and a playground. Restrooms are nearby.

BOATING: Allowed in 3-acre Sunrise Lake. Rowboat and paddle boat rentals are available.

FISHING: Permitted in Sunrise Lake.

SWIMMING: Can be enjoyed in Sunrise Lake. A bathhouse and snack bar are located in the swimming area. For more information, call (973) 267-4351.

HIKING: Four marked trails, along with a portion of the Patriots' Path.

MOUNTAIN BIKING: Permitted on some trails.

HORSEBACK RIDING: Permitted on some trails.

WINTER ACTIVITIES: Cross-country skiing and ice skating.

For additional information:
Morris County Park Commission
53 East Hanover Avenue, P.O. Box 1295
Morristown, NJ 07962–1295
Telephone: (973) 326-7600; Fax: (973) 644-2726

Loantaka Brook Reservation

Kitchell Road ◆ Chatham, Harding, and Morris
Townships ◆ Morris County ◆ 570 acres

LOCATION: Near Fairleigh Dickinson University, southeast of Morristown. From I–287 north, take exit 35, and turn right onto South Street. Proceed one-half mile. Seaton Hackney Stables and Loantaka

Loantaka Brook Reservation.

Loantaka Brook Reservation (Seaton Hackney Stable).

Brook Reservation are on the left, about one-quarter of a mile past Woodland Avenue.

HOURS: Dawn to dusk.

ENTRANCE FEE: None.

HANDICAP ACCESS: None.

SPECIAL FEATURES
  Seaton Hackney Stables—Instruction and boarding. For more information, call (973) 267-1372.

PICNICKING: Tables with grills, drinking water, a playground, and a restroom.

FISHING: Permitted in 6-acre pond.

HIKING: More than five miles of trails, including three marked trails.

HORSEBACK RIDING: Some of the trails at the park are open to horseback riding.

WINTER ACTIVITIES: Cross-country skiing.

For additional information:
Morris County Park Commission
53 East Hanover Avenue, P.O. Box 1295
Morristown, NJ 07962–1295
Telephone: (973) 326-7600; Fax: (973) 644-2726

Mahlon Dickerson Reservation

995 Weldon Road • Jefferson Township, Morris County • 3,000+ acres

LOCATION: From Route 15 (5 miles north of I–80, west of Dover), take Weldon Road northeast approximately 3 miles to the park entrance.

HOURS: The grounds are open from dawn to dusk; the campground office is open Friday through Sunday, from 9:00 A.M. to 5:30 P.M.

ENTRANCE FEE: None.

HANDICAP ACCESS: One of the shelters in the camping area is handicap accessible.

CAMPING: The trailer area has eighteen sites with tables, drinking water, electricity, water hookups, a sanitary dumping station, and restrooms with showers. The tent/Adirondack shelter area has five tent sites with tables and campfire area, and four shelters with tables and campfire area. Pit toilets serve this campground. The shelters can be used when not reserved by groups, for a maximum of fourteen days.

PICNICKING: Numerous sites with grills, drinking water, and restrooms.

FISHING: Permitted at 12-acre Saffin Pond, and at Toomey's Pond.

HIKING: More than twenty miles of trails, including three marked trails.

MOUNTAIN BIKING: Permitted on some trails.

HORSEBACK RIDING: Permitted on some trails.

WINTER ACTIVITIES: Cross-country skiing and ice skating.

> **For additional information:**
> *Mahlon Dickerson Reservation*
> P.O. Box 684
> *Lake Hopatcong, NJ 07849*
> *Telephone: (973) 663-0200; Fax: (973) 663-9636; or*
>
> **Morris County Park Commission**
> P.O. Box 1295
> Morristown, NJ 07962–1295
> *Telephone: (973) 326-7600; Fax: (973) 644-2726*

 # Merrill Creek Reservoir Environmental Preserve

34 Merrill Creek Road ◆ *Washington, Warren County* ◆ *290 acres*

LOCATION: From Route 57, turn north onto Montana Road, approximately 10 miles west of the intersection of Routes 57 and 31.

HOURS: The grounds are open from dawn to dusk. Access to the environmental preserve and boat ramp is gate controlled. The Visitor Center is open seven days a week, year-round, from 8:30 A.M. to 4:30 P.M., except for major holidays.

ENTRANCE FEE: None.

HANDICAP ACCESS: The 0.3-mile Eagle Trail is wheelchair accessible. A floating dock is designed for wheelchair use.

DESCRIPTION: Owned and operated by seven electric utility companies, the reservoir was constructed to store water for release to the

Delaware River during periods of low flow. Surrounding the reservoir are 1,800 acres of forest and field, in addition to a 290-acre wildlife preserve.

SPECIAL FEATURES

Visitor / Education Center—The Visitor Center has hands-on displays, dioramas, and other displays. Pamphlets, brochures, and trail maps are also available.

BOATING: Allowed on the 645-acre lake. Boats must be at least twelve feet in length. They must be launched from the boat ramp, located near the Visitor Center and open during daylight hours. Call for ramp hours during the winter season. Restroom facilities are located at the boat ramp parking area.

FISHING: Permitted from boats and on shore, with the exception of the shoreline of the environmental preserve.

HIKING: Seven marked trails, totaling more than 10 miles, traverse the preserve, including a 5.5-mile trail that circles the perimeter of the reservoir. A trail map is available.

HUNTING: Hunting is permitted under the auspices of the established hunting club, the Merrill Creek Conservation and Sportsmen Association. For more information, call (908) 454-1213; or visit their website at www.merrillcreek.net/MCCSA.html.

WINTER ACTIVITIES: Cross-country skiing.

For additional information:
34 Merrill Creek Road
Washington, NJ 07882
Telephone: (908) 454-1213; Fax: (908) 454-2747;
Website: www.merrillcreek.net

 # Morristown National Historic Park

Morristown, Morris County ◆ 1,698 acres

LOCATION: The park encompasses three separate units. Directions are provided under each unit.

HOURS: The roads and grounds are open from 9:00 A.M. to dusk. Washington's headquarters is open daily, from 9:00 A.M. to 5:00 P.M.

ENTRANCE FEE: Fee charged year-round.

HANDICAP ACCESS: Please see information on each unit.

Children participate in special event at
Morristown National Historic Park.

Jockey Hollow Encampment Area

The largest of the three units, and the site of the visitor center and most of the historic sites and trails. It also includes the New Jersey Brigade encampment area, southwest of Jockey Hollow and adjacent to the Scherman-Hoffman Sanctuaries.

LOCATION: Access to the Jockey Hollow Encampment Area is from I–287, via exit 30B, near Bernardsville, N.J. Turn right onto Route 202 north, and follow the brown and white signs to Jockey Hollow.

HOURS: The Daily Visitor Center is open from 9:00 A.M. to 5:00 P.M.

ENTRANCE FEE: Fee charged.

HANDICAP ACCESS: The Visitor Center is handicap accessible.

SPECIAL FEATURES

Wick House—The historic Wick House was built c. 1750. It served as military headquarters for Major General Arthur St. Clair during the 1779–80 Jockey Hollow Encampment of the Continental Army. Open daily, from 9:30 A.M. to 4:30 P.M.

Pennsylvania Line—Consists of five reproduction Continental Army soldier huts built in the 1960s. They represent a small portion of the huts once located on this site during the 1779–80 Continental Army winter encampment.

HIKING: Twenty-seven miles of day-hike trails, including the Patriots' Path, a hiking trail traversing Morristown National Historic Park and Lewis Morris Park, beginning near the New Jersey Brigade encampment site. The path has numerous parking areas and access points. A trail map is available.

HORSEBACK RIDING: Permitted on twelve miles of trails.

WINTER ACTIVITIES: Cross-country skiing.

Fort Nonsense Area

Site of an earthwork fortification built by Washington's troops in the spring of 1777, on what was then called Kinney's Hill. Its purpose was to protect the main roads leading north and south, and the military storehouses in Morristown. Due to later folklore, the site acquired the name "Fort Nonsense."

LOCATION: Access is either from Western Avenue (in the Jockey Hollow section of the park), or from Washington Street (if entering from Morristown) to Ann Street.

HOURS: Open from 9:00 A.M. to dusk.

ENTRANCE FEE: Not collected at Fort Nonsense. Fees for the entire park are collected at Washington's Headquarters Museum and at the Jockey Hollow Visitor Center.

HANDICAP ACCESS: None.

Washington's Headquarters Area and Adjacent Museum Exhibits

LOCATION: Also in Morristown, about seven miles from Jockey Hollow. Located off I–287, exit 36.

HOURS: Washington's Headquarters Museum is open daily, from 9:00 A.M. to 5:00 P.M.

ENTRANCE FEE: Fee charged.

HANDICAP ACCESS: The Headquarters Museum has limited accessibility for those individuals with mobility impairments. There is a chair lift that can take one between the first and second floors of the museum, but operating it requires assistance from a staff member. The Ford Mansion is not accessible to those with mobility impairments.

SPECIAL FEATURES

Ford Mansion—An original eighteenth-century structure built between 1772 and 1774. It is furnished in the style of the period. The mansion was General Washington's military headquarters for six months during the winter of 1779–80. Guided tours of the Ford Mansion are offered daily.

Washington's Headquarters Museum—Washington's Headquarters Museum was built in 1935. The self-guided museum offers two floors of exhibit galleries, two brief films, an auditorium, and restroom facilities.

For additional information:
30 Washington Place
Morristown, NJ 07960–4299
Visitor Information: (973) 539-2016, ext. 210
Headquarters and Museum: (973) 539-2016
Jockey Hollow Visitor Center: (973) 539-8361 (fax number);
 http://www.nps.gov/morr (website)

 # Musconetcong River
Wildlife Management Area

Warren County • *826 acres*

LOCATION: On the Warren/Hunterdon County line, south of Route 57.

HOURS: Dawn to dusk.

ENTRANCE FEE: None.

HANDICAP ACCESS: None.

BOATING: Car-top access to the Musconetcong River.

FISHING: Permitted in the river.

HUNTING: For deer and small game.

For additional information:
New Jersey Division of Fish and Wildlife
Trenton Office
501 E. State Street, P.O. Box 400
Trenton, NJ 08625–0400
Telephone: (609) 984-0547

 ## Old Troy Park

440 Reynolds Drive ◆ Parsippany-Troy Hills Township ◆
Morris County ◆ 96 acres

LOCATION: North of Route 10, and east of I–287.

HOURS: Dawn to dusk.

ENTRANCE FEE: None.

HANDICAP ACCESS: Picnic tables and some trails are handicap accessible.

PICNICKING: Picnic area with a playground, and a restroom nearby.

FISHING: Permitted in 6-acre pond.

HIKING: Several trails are available.

WINTER ACTIVITIES: Cross-country skiing.

For additional information:
Morris County Park Commission
53 East Hanover Avenue, P.O. Box 1295
Morristown, NJ 07962–1295
Telephone: (973) 326-7600; Fax: (973) 644-2726

 ## Oxford Furnace Lake Park

Kauffman Drive ◆ Oxford Township, Warren County ◆
148 acres

LOCATION: West of Route 31, in the town of Oxford.

HOURS: The grounds are open from dawn to dusk. The swimming area is open from Memorial Day weekend to Labor Day, Monday through Saturday, from 11:30 A.M. to 6:00 P.M., and on Sunday and holidays, from 11:00 A.M. to 7:00 P.M.

ENTRANCE FEE: None.

HANDICAP ACCESS: The playground, picnic area, and restrooms are handicap accessible.

PICNICKING: There is a lightly wooded area with tables, grills, and a playground. Restrooms are seasonal.

BOATING: Allowed in 53-acre Furnace Lake, year-round, electric motors only. There is a ramp for trailer and car-top boats.

FISHING: Permitted in the lake.

SWIMMING: There is lifeguard-supervised swimming in the lake.

For additional information:
Kaufman Drive
Oxford, NJ 07863
Telephone: (908) 453-3098

 Passaic River Park

River Road ◆ Chatham and Long Hill Townships ◆
Morris County ◆ 711 acres

LOCATION: From Route 24 in Chatham, go south on Fairmount Avenue. Continue south to River Road. The park entrance is on the left.

HOURS: Dawn to dusk.

ENTRANCE FEE: None.

HANDICAP ACCESS: None.

PICNICKING: Tables, some with grills.

FISHING: Permitted along five-thousand feet of the Passaic River shoreline.

HIKING: One mile of trails.

WINTER ACTIVITIES: Cross-country skiing and ice skating.

For additional information:
Morris County Park Commission
53 East Hanover Avenue, P.O. Box 1295
Morristown, NJ 07962–1295
Telephone: (973) 326-7600; Fax: (973) 644-2726

 Paulinskill River
Wildlife Management Area

Sussex County ◆ 778 acres

LOCATION: West of Route 519, and east of Swartswood State Park.

HOURS: Dawn to dusk.

ENTRANCE FEE: None.

HANDICAP ACCESS: None.

BOATING: Allowed in 157-acre Paulinskill Lake, with car-top boat access.

FISHING: Permitted in the lake.

HUNTING: For deer, small game, and waterfowl.

For additional information:
New Jersey Division of Fish and Wildlife
Trenton Office
501 E. State Street, P.O. Box 400
Trenton, NJ 08625—0400
Telephone: (609) 984-0547

 # Pequest Wildlife Management Area

Warren County ♦ *4,130 acres*

LOCATION: On Route 46, 9 miles west of Hackettstown.

HOURS: The grounds are open from dawn to dusk. The Pequest Trout Hatchery and Natural Resources Education Center is open on weekdays, from 9:00 A.M. to 4:00 P.M., and on weekends, from 10:00 A.M. to 4:00 P.M.

ENTRANCE FEE: None.

HANDICAP ACCESS: The Education Center, hatchery, and observation area are all handicap accessible.

SPECIAL FEATURES
Pequest Trout Hatchery and Natural Resources Education Center—Interactive exhibits, videos, and films on natural resources; self-guided tour of the facility.

PICNICKING: Tables are available without grills (portable grills are permitted). Restrooms are located in the office, and are open from 8:30 A.M. to 4:30 P.M.

FISHING: Permitted in the Pequest River, which offers some of the better trout fishing in the state.

HIKING: Several marked trails, totaling about six miles.

MOUNTAIN BIKING: Allowed on existing trails and secondary roads from March 1 to April 15, and from June 1 to September 15, as well as on Sundays throughout the year.

HUNTING: For deer, small game, wild turkey, and waterfowl.

WINTER ACTIVITIES: Cross-country skiing on all trails on Sunday.

For additional information:
605 Pequest Road
Oxford, NJ 07863
Telephone: (908) 637-4125

Pyramid Mountain Natural Historical Area

472 Boonton Avenue • Kinnelon Borough and Montville
Township • 1,000+ acres

LOCATION: The Visitor Center is located 3.3 miles north of Main Street, Boonton, on Boonton Avenue (Route 511).

HOURS: The grounds are open from dawn to dusk. The Visitor Center is open Wednesday through Sunday, from 10:00 A.M. to 4:30 P.M.; it is closed in March and December.

ENTRANCE FEE: None.

HANDICAP ACCESS: The Visitor Center is handicap accessible.

SPECIAL FEATURES
Visitor Center—Programs, exhibits, and displays, as well as maps and information. For more information, call (973) 334-3130.

HIKING: More than twenty miles of marked trails.

WINTER ACTIVITIES: Snowshoeing.

For additional information:
Morris County Park Commission
53 East Hanover Avenue, P.O. Box 1295
Morristown, NJ 07962–1295
Telephone: (973) 326-7600; Fax: (973) 644-2726

Rockaway River Wildlife Management Area

Morris County • 2,858 acres

LOCATION: North of Route 80, and east of Route 15, near the town of Woodstock.

HOURS: Dawn to dusk.

ENTRANCE FEE: None.

HANDICAP ACCESS: None.

FISHING: Permitted in the river.

HIKING: Informal trails.

MOUNTAIN BIKING: Allowed on existing trails and secondary roads from March 1 to April 15, and from June 1 to September 15, as well as on all Sundays throughout the year.

HUNTING: For deer, small game, turkey, and waterfowl.

WINTER ACTIVITIES: Cross-country skiing on all trails on Sunday.

> **For additional information:**
> *New Jersey Division of Fish and Wildlife*
> *Trenton Office*
> *501 E. State Street, P.O. Box 400*
> *Trenton, NJ 08625–0400*
> *Telephone: (609) 984-0547*

 # Schooley's Mountain Park

91 Springtown Road ◆ Washington Township,
Morris County ◆ 537 acres

LOCATION: North of Route 24, and west of Route 206. Access to the park is via Camp Washington Road or Springtown Road.

HOURS: The grounds are open from dawn to dusk. Boat rentals are available on weekends, from 11:00 A.M. to 6:00 P.M.

ENTRANCE FEE: None.

HANDICAP ACCESS: Floating dock and ramps have been built to ADA guidelines.

PICNICKING: Wooded and semiwooded sites, with a playground nearby.

BOATING: Rowboat and paddle boat rentals on the 8-acre lake.

FISHING: Permitted in the lake and in the South Branch of the Raritan.

HIKING: Two miles of trails.

HORSEBACK RIDING: Permitted on all trails.

WINTER ACTIVITIES: Cross-country skiing, ice skating, and sledding.

Silas Condict Park

100 Kinnelon Road ◆ Kinnelon Borough, Morris County ◆
265 acres

LOCATION: South of Route 23, and north of the town of Kinnelon. From Kinnelon, take Route 618 (Kinnelon Road) north to Ricker Road.

HOURS: The grounds are open from dawn to dusk. Boat rentals are available from Memorial Day weekend to Labor Day, on weekends only, from 10:30 A.M. to 6:00 P.M.

ENTRANCE FEE: None.

HANDICAP ACCESS: The picnic area, the restroom, and the fishing area are handicap accessible.

PICNICKING: Available at several locations.

BOATING: Paddle boats can be rented on the 10-acre lake. For more information, call (973) 838-0373 (access to this number is seasonal).

FISHING: Permitted in the lake.

HIKING: Several trails, leading to scenic overlooks.

WINTER ACTIVITIES: Cross-country skiing and ice skating.

Sparta Mountain Wildlife Management Area

Sussex County ◆ 1,602 acres

LOCATION: The tract is located off Route 517 and Glen Road, near the town of Sparta.

HOURS: Dawn to dusk.

ENTRANCE FEE: None.

HANDICAP ACCESS: None.

FISHING: Permitted in the lakes and other bodies of water on the tract; 30-acre Ryker Lake is well known for its population of largemouth bass.

HIKING: Informal trails.

MOUNTAIN BIKING: Allowed on existing trails and secondary roads from March 1 to April 15, and from June 1 to September 15, as well as on all Sundays throughout the year.

HUNTING: For deer, small game, turkey, and waterfowl.

WINTER ACTIVITIES: Cross-country skiing on all trails on Sunday.

> **For additional information:**
> New Jersey Division of Fish and Wildlife
> Trenton Office
> 501 E. State Street, P.O. Box 400
> Trenton, NJ 08625–0400
> Telephone: (609) 984-0547

 # Stephens State Park

Morris County ◆ 253 acres

LOCATION: On Willow Grove Street (Route 604), 2 miles east of Hackettstown, or, alternatively, 7.5 miles west of Route 206, on Waterloo Road (Route 604).

HOURS: The grounds are open from dawn to dusk. The park office is open Memorial Day weekend to Labor Day, Monday through Thursday, and Sunday, from 8:00 A.M. to 3:30 P.M., and on Friday and Saturday, from 8:00 A.M. to 8:30 P.M. During the remainder of the year, the park office is open daily, from 8:00 A.M. to 3:30 P.M.

ENTRANCE FEE: None.

HANDICAP ACCESS: The picnic area and the restrooms are handicap accessible.

DESCRIPTION: Located in an attractive setting by the Musconetcong River, this park offers scenic beauty and varied facilities. The area near the office is popular as a background for wedding pictures.

CAMPING: Available from April 1 through October 31. There are forty tent and trailer sites, with modern restrooms and a playground nearby. Each site has a fire ring and a picnic table.

PICNICKING: Several picnic sites, with grills, are located along the Musconetcong River. A playground and restrooms are nearby.

FISHING: Permitted in the Musconetcong River, which provides excellent fishing and is also stocked with trout.

HIKING: Several marked trails and walking paths.

MOUNTAIN BIKING: Permitted on all trails at the park.

HORSEBACK RIDING: Permitted on all trails at the park.

HUNTING: Permitted in designated areas of the park (473 acres), for deer, small game, and turkey.

WINTER ACTIVITIES: Cross-country skiing.

For additional information:
800 Willow Grove Street
Hackettstown, NJ 07840
Telephone: (908) 852-3790

 Stokes State Forest

Sussex County • 15,942 acres

LOCATION: The park office is located off Route 206, 3 miles northwest of Branchville.

HOURS: The grounds are open daily, from 9:00 A.M. to 4 P.M.; the park office is open daily, also from 9:00 A.M. to 4 P.M.

ENTRANCE FEE: A fee is charged for the Stony Lake area from Memorial Day weekend to Labor Day.

HANDICAP ACCESS: Two of the cabins are handicap accessible. The main office is accessible, and the swimming area is partially accessible.

DESCRIPTION: A beautiful example of rugged northern New Jersey forest. Elevations range from 420 to 1,653 feet above sea level. A large number of flowering shrubs and plants can be found throughout the forest, including the beautiful mountain laurel, which is usually in bloom by mid-June.

CABINS: Ten cabins are available for families, varying in size, and sleeping from four to twelve people. Each cabin has a fireplace, a table with benches, chairs, and single- and double-deck bunks. The kitchen has cold running water (one of the cabins has hot water also), an electric refrigerator, and a gas range. Each room has an electric light. All cabins have inside flush toilets. There are no showers. Available from April 1 through December 15.

CAMPING: Three different family camping areas are dispersed throughout the park, with a total of seventy-seven sites. Open all year.

LEAN-TOS: Ten lean-tos have flush toilets, fire rings, and picnic tables nearby. Open all year.

PICNICKING: Available at Stony Lake recreation area and at Kittle Field.

BOATING: Small, nonpowered boats may be launched (car-top access only) at Lake Ocquittunk.

FISHING: Permitted in all of the waters of the forest. Big Flat Brook and its tributaries, annually stocked, provide some of the best trout fishing in the state.

SWIMMING: Available at Stony Lake, with lifeguard supervision during the summer. Restrooms, and a bathhouse with showers, are located at the site. Open Memorial Day weekend to Labor Day.

HIKING: Close to 50 miles of trails, including a 9.3-mile stretch of the Appalachian Trail. A short, self-guided trail traverses Tillman Ravine. A trail map is available.

MOUNTAIN BIKING: Permitted on all trails at the park.

HORSEBACK RIDING: Permitted on all trails at the park.

HUNTING: Permitted in designated areas of the park (14,821 acres), for deer, small game, turkey, and waterfowl.

WINTER ACTIVITIES: Cross-country skiing and snowmobiling (on selected trails).

For additional information:
1 Courson Road
Branchville, NJ 07826
Telephone: (973) 948-3820; Fax: (973) 948-3359

Swartswood State Park

Sussex County • *2,048 acres*

LOCATION: The park office is located off (county road) Route 619, 4 miles north of Newton.

HOURS: The grounds are open from dawn to dusk. The office is open daily, from 9 A.M. to 4 P.M. during the off-season; hours vary during the summer. The boathouse is open, late June through late September, from 6:30 A.M. to 6 P.M. on weekends and holidays, and from 10 A.M. to 6 P.M. on weekdays.

ENTRANCE FEE: Fee charged for day-use area from Memorial Day weekend to Labor Day.

HANDICAP ACCESS: The beach area and boat launches are handicap accessible.

CAMPING: Seventy sites, open April 1 through October 31, are located near Big Swartswood Lake. Each comes with a picnic table and campfire ring. Facilities include modern restrooms with hot showers (open all year), laundry, and a trailer dumping station.

PICNICKING: Tables at both lakes, with grills and restrooms. (Portable toilets only at Little Swartswood.)

BOATING: Boat launches are available at both Big Swartswood Lake and Little Swartswood Lake. Only small electric motors are permitted. Rowboats, canoes, kayaks, and small sailboats can be rented at the boathouse on Big Swartswood Lake. For more information, call (973) 383-4200.

FISHING: Permitted in all bodies of water. Big and Little Swartswood Lakes are stocked annually with trout. Live bait is sold at the boathouse.

SWIMMING: At lifeguard-supervised, sand beach during the summer. Facilities include restrooms with cold showers, changing rooms, and a food concession. Playgrounds and picnic facilities are nearby.

HIKING: Three marked loop trails, totaling five miles, are suitable for day hikes.

MOUNTAIN BIKING: Permitted on all trails.

HUNTING: Permitted in designated areas of the park (978 acres), for deer, small game, turkey, and waterfowl.

WINTER ACTIVITIES: Cross-country skiing and ice fishing.

> **For additional information:**
> P.O. Box 123
> Swartswood, NJ 07877
> Telephone: (973) 383-5230; Fax: (973) 383-7277

 Tourne Park

> 40 McCaffrey Lane ◆ Boonton and Denville Townships ◆
> Morris County ◆ 546 acres

LOCATION: West of I–287, exit 40, and west of the town of Boonton. Access is from both Powerville Road and Old Denville Road. Most facilities are closer to the Powerville Road entrance.

HOURS: Dawn to dusk.

ENTRANCE FEE: None.

HANDICAP ACCESS: The picnic area and playground are handicap accessible.

SPECIAL FEATURES

Eleanor Hinricksen Bird Sanctuary—Features plantings that attract, feed, and provide sanctuary for a wide assortment of birds.

PICNICKING: Several areas, with nonflush toilets.

FISHING: Permitted in the Rockaway River.

MOUNTAIN BIKING: Permitted on trails.

HORSEBACK RIDING: Permitted on some trails.

HIKING: Several hiking and nature trails, including the Hammond Wildflower Trail, a one-mile trail with more than two hundred wildflowers and shrubs, and more than twenty-five species of ferns. This trail is best seen from April through mid-June.

WINTER ACTIVITIES: Cross-country skiing and sledding.

> **For additional information:**
> Morris County Park Commission
> 53 East Hanover Avenue, P.O. Box 1295
> Morristown, NJ 07962–1295
> Telephone: (973) 326-7600; Fax: (973) 644-2726

Trout Brook Wildlife Management Area

Sussex County ◆ *1,098 acres*

LOCATION: West of Route 521 and Swartswood State Park.

HOURS: Dawn to dusk.

ENTRANCE FEE: None.

HANDICAP ACCESS: None.

FISHING: Permitted in the brook.

HIKING: Informal trails.

MOUNTAIN BIKING: Allowed on existing trails and secondary roads from March 1 to April 15, and from June 1 to September 15, as well as on all Sundays throughout the year.

HUNTING: For deer, small game, and turkey.

WINTER ACTIVITIES: Cross-country skiing on all trails on Sunday.

> **For additional information:**
> *New Jersey Division of Fish and Wildlife*
> *Trenton Office*
> *501 E. State Street, P.O. Box 400*
> *Trenton, NJ 08625–0400*
> *Telephone: (609) 984-0547*

 # Wallkill River National Wildlife Refuge

1547 Route 565 ◆ *Vernon Township, Sussex County* ◆ *7,500 acres*

LOCATION: The park office is located east of Route 23, and north of Route 565.

HOURS: The grounds are open from dawn to dusk. The Visitor Center is open weekdays, from 8 A.M. to 4:30 P.M.

ENTRANCE FEE: None.

HANDICAP ACCESS: None.

SPECIAL FEATURES
Visitor Center/Education Center—Wildlife photos and exhibits, and restrooms for public use.

BOATING: Three access points along the river for canoes and kayaks.

FISHING: Two fishing access points along the river. In addition, fishing is allowed from boats.

HIKING: Three marked, self-guided trails open to hikers only. One of the trails is located in a hunting area, and it is suggested that visitors wear safety orange during hunting season.

BIRDWATCHING: Observation tower/blind.

HUNTING: For deer, waterfowl, and turkey.

WINTER ACTIVITIES: Cross-country skiing.

For additional information:
1547 Route 565
Sussex, NJ 07461
Telephone: (973) 702-7266; Fax: (973) 702-7286;
Website: www.wallkillriver.fws.gov

 ## Walpack Wildlife Management Area

Sussex County ◆ 388 acres

LOCATION: Access is from Route 615, approximately 5 miles southwest of Walpack Center.

HOURS: Dawn to dusk.

ENTRANCE FEE: None.

HANDICAP ACCESS: None.

FISHING: Permitted in the Big Flat Brook, which is stocked regularly with trout.

HIKING: Informal trails.

MOUNTAIN BIKING: Allowed on existing trails and secondary roads from March 1 to April 15, and from June 1 to September 15, as well as on all Sundays throughout the year.

HUNTING: For deer, small game, turkey, and waterfowl.

WINTER ACTIVITIES: Cross-country skiing on all trails on Sunday.

For additional information:
New Jersey Division of Fish and Wildlife
Trenton Office
501 E. State Street, P.O. Box 400
Trenton, NJ 08625–0400
Telephone: (609) 984-0547

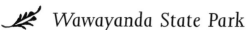

Wawayanda State Park

Sussex and Passaic Counties • *17,541 acres*

LOCATION: The park office is located off Warwick Turnpike, 4 miles north of West Milford.

HOURS: The grounds are open from dawn to dusk. The park office is open daily, from 8:00 A.M. to 4:30 P.M. The boathouse is open seven days a week during the summer, from 6:00 A.M. to 6:00 P.M.; during the month of September and from April through Memorial Day, the boathouse is open only on weekends, from 6:00 A.M. to 6:00 P.M.

ENTRANCE FEE: A fee is charged for the swimming area from Memorial Day weekend to Labor Day.

HANDICAP ACCESS: The swimming area and boat concession are partially handicap accessible. There are two handicap-accessible fishing docks.

DESCRIPTION: Known for its display of rhododendron bloom in late June and early July. The name of the park is the phonetic rendition of the Lenape Indian word meaning "water on the mountain."

PICNICKING: A large picnic area is situated near the swimming area. It has shaded and open spots, with tables and grills. A small playground is located nearby.

BOATING: Allowed in 255-acre Wawayanda Lake. A boathouse with a launching ramp (for trailer and car-top boats) is located a short distance from the bathing beach. Canoes, paddle boats, and rowboats (with or without electric motors) can also be rented. Only electric motors are allowed on the lake. Live bait and fishing supplies are also available. For more information, call (973) 764-1030.

FISHING: Permitted in the lakes throughout the park, for bass, perch, pickerel, and brown and rainbow trout.

SWIMMING: A sandy beach with lifeguard supervision is open from Memorial Day through Labor Day. Restrooms, changing rooms, and a first-aid station are nearby, along with a small concession stand. Inner tubes, rafts, and other flotation devices are not allowed in the swimming area.

HIKING: Twenty-three marked trails, ranging from 0.5 miles to 2.8 miles. The park also has 6 miles of the Appalachian Trail.

MOUNTAIN BIKING: Permitted on some trails.

HORSEBACK RIDING: Permitted on all trails.

HUNTING: Permitted in designated areas of the park (10,984 acres), for deer, small game, turkey, and waterfowl.

WINTER ACTIVITIES: Cross-country skiing, ice fishing, and snowmobiling (on some trails).

> **For additional information:**
> 885 Warwick Turnpike
> Hewitt, NJ 07421
> Telephone: (973) 853-4462; Fax: (973) 853-1383

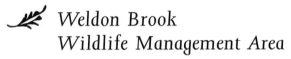

Weldon Brook
Wildlife Management Area

Sussex County ◆ 829 acres

LOCATION: East of Route 15, and west of the town of Milton.

HOURS: Dawn to dusk.

ENTRANCE FEE: None.

HANDICAP ACCESS: None.

FISHING: Permitted in Weldon Brook.

HIKING: Informal trails.

MOUNTAIN BIKING: Allowed on existing trails and secondary roads from March 1 to April 15, and from June 1 to September 15, as well as on all Sundays throughout the year.

HUNTING: For deer, small game, turkey, and waterfowl.

WINTER ACTIVITIES: Cross-country skiing on all trails on Sunday.

> **For additional information:**
> New Jersey Division of Fish and Wildlife
> Trenton Office
> 501 E. State Street, P.O. Box 400
> Trenton, NJ 08625—0400
> Telephone: (609) 984-0547

White Lake Wildlife Management Area

Warren County • 767 acres

LOCATION: North of Route 94, near the town of Marksboro.

HOURS: Dawn to dusk.

ENTRANCE FEE: None.

HANDICAP ACCESS: None.

BOATING: Car-top boat launch.

FISHING: Permitted in 65-acre White Lake.

HIKING: Informal trails.

MOUNTAIN BIKING: Allowed on existing trails and secondary roads from March 1 to April 15, and from June 1 to September 15, as well as on all Sundays throughout the year.

HUNTING: For deer, small game, and turkey.

WINTER ACTIVITIES: Cross-country skiing on all trails on Sunday.

> **For additional information:**
> *New Jersey Division of Fish and Wildlife*
> *Trenton Office*
> *501 E. State Street, P.O. Box 400*
> *Trenton, NJ 08625–0400*
> *Telephone: (609) 984-0547*

Whittingham Wildlife Management Area

Greendell Road • Fredon and Green Townships,
Sussex County • 1,930 acres

LOCATION: Take Route 206 in Newton to Route 519 south. Turn east onto Greendell Road (Route 319), where you will find the office.

HOURS: Dawn to dusk.

ENTRANCE FEE: None.

HANDICAP ACCESS: None.

FISHING: There is limited fishing in the Pequest River, which is stocked with trout.

HIKING: Informal trails.

MOUNTAIN BIKING: Allowed on existing trails and secondary roads from March 1 to April 15, and from June 1 to September 15, as well as on all Sundays throughout the year.

HORSEBACK RIDING: Allowed on all trails with the required permit.

HUNTING: For deer, small game, turkey, and waterfowl.

WINTER ACTIVITIES: Cross-country skiing on all trails on Sunday.

> **For additional information:**
> *New Jersey Division of Fish and Wildlife*
> *Trenton Office*
> *501 E. State Street, P.O. Box 400*
> *Trenton, NJ 08625–0400*
> *Telephone: (609) 984-0547*

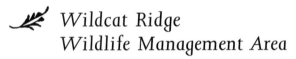

Wildcat Ridge Wildlife Management Area

Morris County ◆ *2,777 acres*

LOCATION: The tract is bisected by Route 513 (Upper Hibernia Road), north of Route 80.

HOURS: Dawn to dusk.

ENTRANCE FEE: None.

HANDICAP ACCESS: None.

SPECIAL FEATURES

Visitor Center/Education Center—A small house near the hawk watch serves as an interpretive center, but has limited hours of operation. It has information on trails. Nearby is a public-use composting toilet.

HIKING: Informal trails.

BIRDWATCHING: An official hawk-watch platform is located at the top of the ridge. For additional information, contact the Hawk Migration Association of North America at: www.hmana.org.

MOUNTAIN BIKING: Allowed on existing trails and secondary roads from March 1 to April 15, and from June 1 to September 15, as well as on all Sundays throughout the year.

HUNTING: For deer, small game, turkey, and waterfowl.

WINTER ACTIVITIES: Cross-country skiing on all trails on Sunday.

For additional information:
New Jersey Division of Fish and Wildlife
Trenton Office
501 E. State Street, P.O. Box 400
Trenton, NJ 08625–0400
Telephone: (609) 984-0547

Worthington State Forest

Old Mine Road ◆ Delaware Water Gap, Warren County ◆
6,233 acres

LOCATION: The park office is located off Old Mine Road, 3 miles north of the Water Gap.

HOURS: The grounds are open from dawn to dusk. The office is open daily, from 8:00 A.M. to 4:30 P.M. During the summer, the office is often open on the weekends from 8:00 A.M. to 10:00 P.M.

ENTRANCE FEE: None.

HANDICAP ACCESS: Fishing, the boat-ramp area, campsites (to varying degrees), and restrooms are handicap accessible.

DESCRIPTION: Running along the crest of the Kittatinny Mountain ridge, this tract offers some of the most rugged terrain found in New Jersey, with elevations ranging from 200 feet at the Delaware River, to 1,480 feet at the highest point.

CAMPING: Seventy-seven sites for tents or trailers are situated along the Delaware River, each with a table and fire ring. All have access to modern toilets and hot showers. Camping is available from April 1 through December 31. There are no water, electric, or sewer connections for trailers.

BOATING: Allowed in the Delaware River. A boat ramp is located near the park office. There are no restrictions on boat type, though jet skis are not permitted.

FISHING: Permitted in the Delaware River and in Dunnfield Creek. Dunnfield Creek has been designated a "Wild Trout Stream" because it supports a natural population of trout.

HIKING: Nine marked trails, ranging from 1.1 miles to 3.5 miles. The park also includes a 7.8-mile stretch of the Appalachian Trail.

HUNTING: Permitted in designated areas of the park (5,351 acres), for deer, small game, turkey, and waterfowl.

WINTER ACTIVITIES: Cross-country skiing.

For additional information:

HC 62, Box 2,
Columbia, NJ 07832
Telephone: (908) 841-9575

Region Two

Bergen, Essex, Hudson, Passaic, & Union Counties

Greg Johnson

Long Pond Iron Works State Park.

PASSAIC

BERGEN

MAHWAH

WANAQUE

WYCKOFF

PATERSON

PARAMUS

TENAFLY

HACKENSACK

MONTCLAIR

ESSEX

JERSEY CITY

NEWARK

MILBURN

HUDSON

ELIZABETH

BAYONNE

UNION

- # Parks
- • Selected Towns
- Selected Roads
- County Borders

0   5
miles

1   Abram S. Hewitt State Forest
2   Branch Brook Park
3   Brookdale Park
4   Campgaw Mountain Reservation
5   Cora Hartshorn Arboretum and Bird Sanctuary
6   Darlington County Park
7   Eagle Rock Reservation
8   Echo Lake Park
9   Flat Rock Brook
10 Garrett Mountain Reservation
11 Goffle Brook Park
12 James A. McFaul Wildlife Center
13 James J. Braddock—North Hudson Park
14 Liberty State Park
15 Lincoln Park
16 Long Pond Iron Works State Park
17 Mills Reservation
18 Newark Pequannock Watershed
19 Norvin Green State Park
20 Palisades Interstate Park
21 Pascack Brook County Park
22 Passaic River Park
23 Rahway River Park
24 Ramapo Mountain State Forest
25 Ramapo Valley County Reservation
26 Richard W. Dekorte Park
27 Rifle Camp Park
28 Ringwood State Park
29 Riverside County Park
30 Saddle River County Park
31 Samuel Nelkin County Park
32 Sawmill Creek Wildlife Management Area
33 South Mountain Reservation
34 Stephen R. Gregg Park
35 Tenafly Nature Center
36 Van Saun County Park
37 Verona Park
38 Wanaque Wildlife Management Area
39 Warinanco Park
40 Watchung Reservation
41 Weequahic County Park
42 Weis Ecology Center
43 West Essex County Park
44 Wood Dale County Park

Abram S. Hewitt State Forest

Warwick Turnpike ◆ West Milford Township,
Passaic County ◆ 2,001 acres

LOCATION: Abram S. Hewitt State Forest is located in Vernon Township, off of Warwick Turnpike. The forest can be reached by taking Route 23 to Union Valley Road, into West Milford. At the light past the town hall, bear left and continue on Union Valley Road. At the next fork in the road, turn left onto White Road and, at the next inter-section, turn right. Parking is along both sides of Warwick Turn-pike. Trails start near the stream.

HOURS: Dawn to dusk.

ENTRANCE FEE: None.

HANDICAP ACCESS: None.

HIKING: Six marked trails, totaling 10 miles, including 3.4 miles of the Appalachian Trail. Trail heads are located on Warwick Turnpike, east of Union Valley Road, and on Route 511, just south of the New Jersey-New York border. A trail map is available.

HORSEBACK RIDING: Permitted on trails.

HUNTING: Permitted in designated areas of the park (1,941 acres), for deer, small game, and turkey.

WINTER ACTIVITIES: Cross-country skiing.

For additional information:
c/o Wawayanda State Forest
885 Warwick Turnpike
Hewitt, NJ 07421
Telephone: (973) 853-4462

Branch Brook Park

Lake Street ◆ Newark, Essex County ◆ 360 acres

LOCATION: North of I–280, and east of the Garden State Parkway. Park Avenue, Heller Parkway, and Bloomfield Avenue (Route 506) cut through the park.

HOURS: Dawn to dusk.

Greg Johnson

Branch Brook Park.

Branch Brook Park.

ENTRANCE FEE: None.

HANDICAP ACCESS: None.

DESCRIPTION: This large, urban park has the distinction of being the first county park in the United States.

SPECIAL FEATURES

Japanese Cherry Trees—This park has the largest display of Japanese cherry trees in the country—more than three thousand trees. The trees are usually in bloom by mid-April.

PICNICKING: Tables, no grills. Restrooms nearby.

FISHING: Permitted in the 24-acre lake, and in the river that flows through the park.

HIKING: Walking paths.

> **For additional information:**
> Essex County Department of Parks, Recreation & Cultural Affairs
> 115 Clifton Avenue
> Newark, NJ 07104
> Telephone: (973) 268-3500

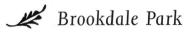

Brookdale Park

Bellevue Avenue ◆ Bloomfield and Montclair,
Essex County ◆ *121 acres*

LOCATION: West of the Garden State Parkway, exit 151. Access is from Watchung Avenue in Bloomfield, or from Grove Street in Montclair.

HOURS: Dawn to dusk.

ENTRANCE FEE: None.

HANDICAP ACCESS: None.

SPECIAL FEATURES
Formal Rose Garden—More than twelve hundred rose bushes of 140 varieties.

FISHING: Permitted in 1-acre pond.

HIKING: Seven miles of walking paths.

> **For additional information:**
> *Essex County Department of Parks, Recreation & Cultural Affairs*
> *115 Clifton Avenue*
> *Newark, NJ 07104*
> *Telephone: (973) 268-3500*

Campgaw Mountain Reservation

Campgaw Road ◆ *Mahwah, Bergen County* ◆ *1,351 acres*

LOCATION: East of Route 202 (Ramapo Valley Road), and north of Route 208.

HOURS: Dawn to dusk.

ENTRANCE FEE: None.

HANDICAP ACCESS: The restroom is handicap accessible.

SPECIAL FEATURES
Saddle Ridge Riding Center—Lessons, boarding and rental of horses, and organized trail rides. People with their own horses may ride on the 28 acres available at the center or on other nearby land, but not at Campgaw Park. For more information, call (201) 847-9999.

CAMPING: Allowed from April 1 through November 30. Campsites with tables and fire pits are available in a wooded area. Some sites have simple shelters. Modern bathroom facilities with showers are located nearby. For more information, call (201) 327-3500.

PICNICKING: There is a picnic area with a restroom.

FISHING: Permitted in 3-acre Campgaw Pond; catch and release.

HIKING: Marked trails with map.

WINTER ACTIVITIES: Cross-country skiing and skiing. For more information, visit www.skicampgaw.com.

> **For additional information:**
> Bergen County Department of Parks
> One Bergen County Plaza, 4th floor
> Hackensack, NJ 07601—7076
> Telephone: (201) 336-7275; Fax: 201 336-7262

 # Cora Hartshorn Arboretum and Bird Sanctuary

Short Hills, Union County • 16.5 acres

LOCATION: From Route 24, take the exit marked Hobart Avenue (north). At the top of the ramp, turn right. Go two blocks, and turn right at the blinker. Proceed 0.75 miles, and turn right onto Forest Drive. Go under the railroad tracks, and cross Chatham Road. The arboretum will be on the left.

HOURS: The grounds are open from dawn to dusk. The Stone House is open Monday through Friday, from 9:00 A.M. to 4:00 P.M., and on Saturday, from 10:00 A.M. to 11:30 A.M., during the school year.

ENTRANCE FEE: None.

HANDICAP ACCESS: None.

SPECIAL FEATURES

Visitor/Education Center—A structure known as the Stone House has natural history displays. Restrooms are available.

HIKING: More than three miles of trails. Trail map is available.

BIRDWATCHING: Can be enjoyed at bird feeders outside of the Stone House.

> **For additional information:**
> 324 Forest Drive South
> Short Hills, NJ 07078
> Telephone: (973) 376-3587; Fax: (973) 379-5059
> *Website:* www.hartshornarboretum.com

Darlington County Park

600 Darlington Avenue ◆ *Mahwah, Bergen County* ◆
178 acres

LOCATION: Take Route 202 (Ramapo Valley Road) to Darlington Avenue.

HOURS: The grounds are open from dawn to dusk. The park office is open Monday through Friday, from 9:00 A.M. to 4:00 P.M. Swimming is available from Memorial Day weekend until mid-June, Friday through Sunday, from 10:00 A.M. to 6:00 P.M., and from mid-June until Labor Day, daily, from 10:00 A.M. to 6:00 P.M.

ENTRANCE FEE: Fee charged for park entrance from Memorial Day through Labor Day.

HANDICAP ACCESS: Ramps with handrails make the swimming beach handicap accessible. The restrooms and picnic area are also accessible.

PICNICKING: Picnic grove, with a playground and a restroom.

SWIMMING: There is lifeguard-supervised swimming at two lakes with sand beaches. Both have restrooms, a snack bar, changing facilities, a first-aid station, and playgrounds. For more information, call (201) 327-3500.

FISHING: Permitted in the 18-acre lake.

WINTER ACTIVITIES: Cross-country skiing.

For additional information:
Bergen County Department of Parks
One Bergen County Plaza, 4th floor
Hackensack, NJ 07601–7076
Telephone: (201) 336-7275; Fax: (201) 336-7262

 # Eagle Rock Reservation

Eagle Rock Avenue ◆ *West Orange, Essex County* ◆
408 acres

LOCATION: South of Route 506, and east of Route 577 (Prospect Avenue), west of Montclair.

HOURS: Dawn to dusk.

ENTRANCE FEE: None.

HANDICAP ACCESS: None.

PICNICKING: Tables, some with fireplaces, and portable toilets.

HIKING: Three and a half miles of foot trails.

HORSEBACK RIDING: Seven miles of trails.

> **For additional information:**
> Essex County Department of Parks, Recreation & Cultural Affairs
> 115 Clifton Avenue
> Newark, NJ 07104
> Telephone: (973) 268-3500

 ## Echo Lake Park

Mountainside and Westfield ◆ *Union County* ◆ *144 acres*

LOCATION: From I–287, take exit 57. Follow Skyline Drive to Route 511 (Greenwood Lake Turnpike). Turn right, and travel approximately 5 miles. Or, from Route 23, take Union Valley Road (Route 513) approximately 6 miles, and bear right onto Marshall Hill Road, which becomes Greenwood Lake Turnpike (Route 511). Parking is available at the north boat ramp, at Beech Road, and at historic district parking lots.

HOURS: Dawn to dusk.

ENTRANCE FEE: None.

HANDICAP ACCESS: A fishing dock at one of the three lakes is handicap accessible, and there are accessible tables at the picnic area.

PICNICKING: Tables with grills. There are portable toilets.

FISHING: Permitted in three small lakes.

WINTER ACTIVITIES: Sledding (Springfield Avenue entrance) and ice skating.

> **For additional information:**
> Union County Department of Parks and Recreation
> Administration Building
> Elizabeth, NJ 07207
> Telephone: (908) 527-4900

 ## Flat Rock Brook

Englewood, Bergen County ◆ *150 acres*

LOCATION: Off Route 4, east of Route 501, and south of Route 505.

HOURS: The grounds are open from dawn to dusk. The building hours are Tuesday through Friday, from 9:00 A.M. to 5:00 P.M., and on Saturday and Sunday, from 1:00 P.M. to 5:00 P.M.

ENTRANCE FEE: None.

HANDICAP ACCESS: The 900-foot boardwalk trail is handicap accessible.

DESCRIPTION: Operated by the Flat Rock Brook Nature Association (a membership organization), the area is maintained as a sanctuary for animal and plant life and is a center for environmental education.

SPECIAL FEATURES
Visitor Center—Exhibits and displays of natural history, as well as of small animals. Restroom available during open hours.

PICNICKING: Parking for the picnic area is on Jones Road. This area has tables (fires not permitted), a playground, and a restroom. Open Memorial Day weekend to Labor Day, from 9:00 A.M. to 5:00 P.M.

HIKING: Six marked trails, totaling 3.2 miles. A trail map is available.

WINTER ACTIVITIES: Cross-country skiing.

For additional information:
443 Van Nostrand Avenue
Englewood, NJ 07631
Telephone: (201) 567-1265; Fax: (201) 567-0399;
Website: www.flatrockbrook.org

 # Garrett Mountain Reservation

Valley Road ◆ *Paterson, Passaic County* ◆ *569 acres*

LOCATION: South of I–80, west of Route 19, and southwest of Paterson.

HOURS: The grounds are open from dawn to dusk. Lambert Castle Museum is open Wednesday through Sunday, from 1:00 P.M. to 4:00 P.M. The Equestrian Center is open spring through summer, Saturday through Monday, from 9:00 A.M. to 6:00 P.M., and Tuesday through Friday, from 9:00 A.M. to 9:00 P.M. During the winter, the center is open Monday, from 9:00 A.M. to 7:00 P.M.

ENTRANCE FEE: None.

HANDICAP ACCESS: The fishing area is handicap accessible. The Equestrian Center gives horseback riding lessons to handicapped children.

Lambert Castle—A national historic landmark. It contains a museum run by the Passaic County Historical Society, on local and regional history. Fee charged for admission. For more information, call (973) 247-0085.

Garret Mountain Equestrian Center—Lessons are available at the center, and there are also trail lessons. For more information, call (973) 279-2974.

PICNICKING: Several areas, with tables and grills. Restrooms are nearby.

FISHING: Permitted in 12-acre Barbours Pond, stocked with trout.

HIKING: Informal trails.

HORSEBACK RIDING: Permitted on trails; contact Equestrian Center for details.

For additional information:
Passaic County Parks Department
311 Pennsylvania Avenue
Paterson, NJ 07503
Telephone: (973) 881-4832

 # Goffle Brook Park

Goffle Road ◆ *Hawthorne, Passaic County* ◆
103 acres

LOCATION: From Route 208 northwest, in the vicinity of Hawthorne, turn left onto Goffle Road, heading south.

HOURS: Dawn to dusk.

ENTRANCE FEE: None.

HANDICAP ACCESS: Picnic tables and a playground for the disabled.

PICNICKING: Picnic area with grills, a playground, and a restroom.

FISHING: Permitted in 5-acre pond, and also in Goffle Brook.

For additional information:
Passaic County Parks Department
311 Pennsylvania Avenue
Paterson, NJ 07503
Telephone: (973) 881-4832

James A. McFaul Wildlife Center

Crescent Avenue ◆ *Wyckoff, Bergen County* ◆ *81 acres*

LOCATION: Take Route 4 west to Route 208, to Goffle Road. Go north on Goffle Road, to Goodwin Avenue. Continue on for about one-quarter of a mile, to Crescent Avenue. Turn right onto Crescent Avenue.

HOURS: The grounds are open from dawn to dusk. The Wildlife Center is open weekdays, from 8:00 A.M. to 4:45 P.M., and on weekends and holidays, from 1:00 P.M. to 4:45 P.M.

ENTRANCE FEE: None.

HANDICAP ACCESS: Easy access to the center's displays and live animals. A Braille guide to the nature walk is available. The boardwalk trail is handicap accessible.

SPECIAL FEATURES

Wildlife Center—The Wildlife Center has a spring display of 25,000 daffodils. It also has live displays of snakes and turtles, and two large aquariums, one freshwater and one saltwater. Outside are live animals and an observatory, overlooking a pond, for waterfowl. A restroom is located inside the center. For more information, call (201) 891-5571.

HIKING: A trail winds for two-thirds of a mile through a diverse terrain of wooded areas, streams, and a small swamp. Self-guiding booklet available.

BIRDWATCHING: From the observation area inside or outside, overlooking the pond.

For additional information:
Bergen County Department of Parks
One Bergen County Plaza, 4th floor
Hackensack, NJ 07601–7076
Telephone: (201) 336-7275; Fax: (201) 336-7262

 # James J. Braddock—North Hudson Park

Kennedy Boulevard ◆ *North Bergen, Hudson County* ◆
167 acres

LOCATION: Off Route 501, north of Guttenberg.

HOURS: The grounds are open from dawn to dusk; the park office is open year-round, Monday through Friday, from 8:00 A.M. to 4:00 P.M.

ENTRANCE FEE: None.

HANDICAP ACCESS: None.

DESCRIPTION: The park was established in 1910, and the lake is the largest in Hudson County. The park is built on the highest ground in the county and affords a view of the New York skyline, the Palisades, and the Hudson River.

PICNICKING: Tables, no grills, with a playground and a restroom.

FISHING: Permitted in 15-acre Woodcliff Lake.

> **For additional information:**
> Hudson County Parks and Recreation
> Administration Building, Lincoln Park
> Jersey City, NJ 07304
> Telephone: (201) 915-1386; Park office: (201) 319-3747;
>   Fax: (201) 915-1385

✎ Liberty State Park

Hudson County • 1,212 acres

LOCATION: Access is from exit 14B, off of the New Jersey Turnpike. Follow signs.

HOURS: The grounds are open from dawn to dusk; the office is open daily, from 8:00 A.M. to 6:00 P.M. The Interpretive Center is open daily during the summer, from 9:00 A.M. to 4:00 P.M., and is otherwise open Monday through Saturday, from 9:00 A.M. to 4:00 P.M.

ENTRANCE FEE: None.

HANDICAP ACCESS: The railroad terminal, the offices, the Interpretive Center, the Science Center, the picnic area, and the fishing area are handicap accessible.

DESCRIPTION: Important during the great European migrations as a transportation hub, the formerly abandoned land has been cleaned up and developed for public recreational use.

SPECIAL FEATURES

Central Railroad of New Jersey Terminal—Built in 1889, the terminal served between 30,000 and 50,000 commuters a day by 1915. Closed in 1967, it is now partially restored and is open during the summer months and for special events.

Interpretive Center—Exhibits that focus on the habitat of the Hudson River and the surrounding area. For more information, call (201) 915-3409.

Liberty Science Center—Hands-on museum of science and technology. For more information, call (201) 200-1000, or visit http://www.lsc.org/.

PICNICKING: Located at the southern end of the park, near the administration building. There are no grills. A restroom is located nearby.

BOATING: A launching ramp that accommodates trailers and car-top boats is open year-round during daylight hours. It offers access to the Hudson River and nearby Atlantic Ocean.

FISHING: The Hudson River offers excellent fishing for bluefish, shad, and striped bass. Access from Liberty walkway.

CRABBING: Permitted in the river. Access from Liberty walkway.

HIKING: Nature trails in the 60-acre natural area that consists mostly of salt marsh.

For additional information:
Morris Pesin Drive
Jersey City, NJ 07305
Telephone: (201) 915-3403

 # Lincoln Park

Jersey City, Hudson County ◆ *273 acres*

LOCATION: Off Route 501 (Kennedy Boulevard), west of Jersey City.

HOURS: The grounds are open from dawn to dusk; the park office is open year-round, Monday through Friday, from 8:00 A.M. to 4:00 P.M.

ENTRANCE FEE: None.

HANDICAP ACCESS: None.

PICNICKING: Tables, no grills, with a playground and restrooms.

FISHING: Permitted in 3-acre Lincoln Park Lake.

HIKING: Nature trails.

For additional information:
Hudson County Parks and Recreation
Administration Building, Lincoln Park
Jersey City, NJ 07304
Telephone: (201) 915-1386; Fax: (201) 915-1385;
    Park office: (973) 694-1146

 # Long Pond Iron Works State Park

Route 511, Passaic County • 2,591 acres

LOCATION: On Route 511, on the border between West Milford Township and Ringwood Boro, north of Wanaque.

HOURS: The grounds are open from dawn to dusk. The boat ramps are open twenty-four hours a day, seven days a week.

ENTRANCE FEE: None.

HANDICAP ACCESS: None.

SPECIAL FEATURES
Long Pond Ironworks Museum—Dedicated to preserving and restoring this unique eighteenth- and nineteenth-century industrial site and village, and to interpreting its history. The museum is open April through November, Saturday and Sunday, from 1:00 P.M. to 4:00 P.M. For more information, call (973) 657-1688.

PICNICKING: None.

BOATING: Trailer and car-top boat launches. Electric and gas motors (up to 10 horsepower) are permitted.

FISHING: Permitted in 505-acre Monksville Reservoir for muskellunge, walleye, bass, and trout.

HIKING: Marked and unmarked trails.

MOUNTAIN BIKING: Permitted on trails.

HORSEBACK RIDING: Permitted on trails.

HUNTING: Permitted in designated areas of the park (1,673 acres), for deer, small game, turkey, and waterfowl.

WINTER ACTIVITIES: Cross-country skiing and ice fishing.

For additional information:
c/o Ringwood State Park
1304 Sloatsburg Road
Ringwood, NJ 07456–1799
Telephone: (973) 962-7031

 Mills Reservation
========

Cedar Grove, Essex County ♦ 157 acres

LOCATION: From the Garden State Parkway, take exit 151 (Watchung Avenue, Montclair). Turn west from the exit ramp onto Watchung Avenue, and drive about 2 miles until the road ends at Upper Montclair Avenue. Turn north, and go 1.7 miles to the traffic light at Normal Avenue. Turn west, and drive 0.3 miles to the entrance on the left.

HOURS: Dawn to dusk.

ENTRANCE FEE: None.

HANDICAP ACCESS: None.

HIKING: Three miles of trails.

HORSEBACK RIDING: Permitted on trails.

For additional information:
Essex County Department of Parks, Recreation & Cultural Affairs
115 Clifton Avenue
Newark, NJ 07104
Telephone: (973) 268-3500

 Newark Pequannock Watershed
========

Morris, Passaic, and Sussex Counties ♦ 35,000 acres

LOCATION: The office is located on Echo Lake Road in Newfoundland, east of Route 513.

HOURS: The grounds are open from dawn to dusk. The watershed office is open year-round, Monday through Friday, from 8:00 A.M. to 4:00 P.M.; in April through October, it is also open on Saturday, from 8:00 A.M. to 12:30 P.M.

ENTRANCE FEE: Fee charged for various permits.

HANDICAP ACCESS: None.

BOATING: Ramps for trailer and car-top boats are located at Echo Lake (300 acres), Canistear Reservoir (350 acres), Clinton Reservoir (423 acres), and Oak Ridge Reservoir (482 acres). Electric motors only. Permit required from the NWCDC.

FISHING: Allowed in all four bodies of water. Permit required from the NWCDC.

HIKING: Miles of marked and unmarked trails. Permit required from the NWCDC.

HORSEBACK RIDING: Miles of marked trails. Permit required from the NWCDC.

HUNTING: Allowed in designated areas. Permit required from the NWCDC.

> **For additional information:**
> NWCDC
> 40 Clinton Street, 4th floor
> Newark, NJ 07102
> Telephone: (973) 622-4521
>   or
> 223 Echo Lake Road
> P.O. Box 319
> Newfoundland, NJ 07435
> Telephone: (973) 697-2850

 # Norvin Green State Forest

Bloomingdale, Passaic County • 4,365 acres

LOCATION: Take I–287 to exit 57. Follow Skyline Drive to Greenwood Lake Turnpike, to West Brook Road, to Snake Den Road. Follow signs to Weis Ecology Center. Parking is available at Weis Ecology Center, or along Burnt Meadow Road and Glen Wild Road.

HOURS: Dawn to dusk.

ENTRANCE FEE: None.

HANDICAP ACCESS: None.

BOATING: Walk-in access for canoes and small boats. Electric motors only.

FISHING: Permitted in 15-acre Lake Sonoma.

HIKING: Miles of marked and unmarked trails.

MOUNTAIN BIKING: Permitted on some trails.

HORSEBACK RIDING: Permitted on some trails.

HUNTING: Permitted in designated areas of the park (2,455 acres), for deer, small game, turkey, and waterfowl.

WINTER ACTIVITIES: Cross-country skiing and ice fishing.

For additional information:
c/o Ringwood State Park
1304 Sloatsburg Road
Ringwood, NJ 07456–1799
Telephone: (973) 962-7031

Palisades Interstate Park

Bergen County ♦ 2,500 acres

Alpine Area

LOCATION: From Palisades Interstate Parkway, northbound, take exit 2 (heading toward Route 2, Route 9W, Alpine, Closter). When getting off of the exit, stay straight, passing the park headquarters. Follow a long, narrow road down a hill. Almost at the river, make

Palisades Interstate Park.

a three-quarter turn around a small circle, and continue the rest of the way down to parking.

HOURS: Dawn to dusk.

ENTRANCE FEE: Parking fee charged Memorial Day weekend to Labor Day, during weekends and holidays.

HANDICAP ACCESS: Restrooms and a picnic area are handicap accessible.

DESCRIPTION: Established in 1900, the Palisades Interstate Park Commission oversees and protects more than 80,000 acres in New Jersey and New York. The 2,500-acre New Jersey section has been named both a national historic landmark and a national natural landmark.

SPECIAL FEATURES

Kearney House—Dating from around 1760, this restored building is currently a museum of area history from Revolutionary times to the early 1900s. Open from May through October, on weekends and holidays, from 12:00 P.M. to 5:00 P.M., or by appointment.

PICNICKING: Available, with nearby playground and restroom, as well as a public phone, drinking water, and vending machines. No grills are provided; visitors must bring their own.

BOATING: Car-top boats can be launched at the beach at the northern end of the area.

FISHING: Permitted along seawalls and shoreline of the Hudson River for catfish, striped bass, white perch, and eels.

CRABBING: Permitted along seawalls and shoreline of the Hudson River.

HIKING: The park's trail system totals thirty miles of trails.

Englewood Area (Englewood Cliffs)

LOCATION: From Palisades Interstate Parkway, take exit 1, Palisades Avenue. Turn left. Enter the park, and follow the road down to the river.

HOURS: Dawn to dusk.

ENTRANCE FEE: Parking fee charge from May through October on weekends and holidays; from Memorial Day weekend to Labor Day, on Wednesday through Friday.

HANDICAP ACCESS: Restrooms and picnic areas are handicap accessible.

PICNICKING: Available, with a playground and restrooms nearby. No grills are provided; visitors must bring their own.

BOATING: Car-top boats may be launched from Bloomers Beach.

FISHING: Permitted along seawalls and shoreline of the Hudson River for catfish, striped bass, white perch, and eels.

CRABBING: Permitted along seawalls and shoreline of the Hudson River.

HIKING: The park's trail system totals thirty miles.

Fort Lee Historic Park

Hudson Terrace (Fort Lee)

LOCATION: From Routes 4, 46, 80 and 95, take exit for Fort Lee/ Palisades Interstate Parkway. Continue on Bridge Plaza South, headed east, past several traffic lights. At the last light, turn right onto Bigler Street; go to end of the block, which is Main Street. Turn left (east) on Main, and then bear left (north) on Hudson Terrace. The park entrance is on the right, immediately before the traffic light.

Fort Lee Historic Park (Palisades Interstate Park).

HOURS: The grounds are open from dawn to dusk. The Visitor Center is open March 1 through December 31, Wednesday to Sunday, from 10 A.M. to 5:00 P.M.; and in January and February, on Saturday and Sunday, from 10:00 A.M. to 5:00 P.M.

ENTRANCE FEE: Fee charged from Memorial Day weekend through Labor Day, on weekends and holidays. Call to confirm hours.

HANDICAP ACCESS: The main floor of the Visitor Center and Museum is handicap accessible.

SPECIAL FEATURES

Visitor/Education Center—Provides information on the role of Fort Lee in the American Revolution, focusing on the story of how George Washington was forced to evacuate the area in November 1776, and begin his famous retreat through New Jersey. For more information, call (201) 461-1776.

PICNICKING: Permitted, no barbeques.

HIKING: Three miles of paved walkways.

Hazzard's Boat Launching Ramp

Fort Lee ◆ *Telephone: (201) 768-1360*

LOCATION: Beneath the George Washington Bridge, access through Ross Dock area.

HOURS: Open daily from May 1 through October 31, dawn to dusk; in November through March, open to foot traffic only.

ENTRANCE FEE: Fee charged to launch boats.

HANDICAP ACCESS: The boat ramp is handicap accessible.

BOATING: Trailer boats of up to 24 feet, as well as car-top.

Ross Dock

LOCATION: From Routes 4, 46, 80 and 95, take exit for Fort Lee/Palisades Interstate Parkway. Continue on Bridge Plaza South, headed east, past several traffic lights. At the last light, turn right onto Bigler Street; go to the end of the block, which is Main Street. Turn left (east) on Main, and then bear right (south) at River Road. The park entrance is on the left. Follow Henry Hudson Drive about 1 mile to the circle; the entrance to the area is off the circle.

HOURS: Open daily from the first weekend in April through the last weekend in October, dawn to dusk. From November through March, there is foot access only.

ENTRANCE FEE: Parking fee charged from May through October on weekdays; and from Memorial Day weekend to Labor Day, on weekends and holidays.

HANDICAP ACCESS: Restrooms and picnic areas are handicap accessible.

PICNICKING: Available, with a playground and restrooms. A telephone and drinking water are nearby. Some grills provided.

FISHING: Permitted along seawalls and shoreline of the Hudson River for catfish, striped bass, white perch, and eels.

CRABBING: Permitted along seawalls and shoreline of the Hudson River.

HIKING: The park's trail system totals thirty miles.

State Line Lookout

LOCATION: From Palisades Interstate Parkway, northbound, take exit for State Line Lookout, which is about 2 miles north of exit 2.

HOURS: The grounds are open from dawn to dusk. Lookout Inn is generally open weekdays, from 11:00 A.M. to one hour before dusk, and on weekends, from 9:00 A.M. to one-half hour before dusk.

ENTRANCE FEE: None.

HANDICAP ACCESS: Lookout Inn, restrooms, and an overlook are handicap accessible.

SPECIAL FEATURES
Lookout Inn—A snack bar, book and gift shop, and information center.

HIKING: The park's trail system totals thirty miles.

WINTER ACTIVITIES: Five marked cross-country ski trails, totaling nine miles. Map available.

For additional information:
P.O. Box 155
Alpine, NJ 07620
Telephone: (201) 768-1360; Fax: (201) 767-3842;
Website: www.www.njpalisades.org

 ## Pascack Brook County Park

Emerson Road ✦ *Westwood, Bergen County* ✦ *137 acres*

LOCATION: North of Route 502 (Old Hook Road), and east of Route 503 (Kinderkamack Road).

HOURS: Dawn to dusk.

ENTRANCE FEE: None.

HANDICAP ACCESS: None.

PICNICKING: Tables, with a playground and restrooms nearby.

FISHING: Permitted in the pond.

WINTER ACTIVITIES: Ice skating.

For additional information:
Bergen County Department of Parks
One Bergen County Plaza, 4th floor
Hackensack, NJ 07601–7076
Telephone: (201) 336-7275; Fax: (201) 336-7262

Passaic River Park

Springfield Avenue ✦ *Berkeley Heights Township, and*
Borough of New Providence ✦ *Union County* ✦ *285 acres*

LOCATION: This linear park is located north of Route 512 (Springfield Avenue), along the Passaic River, and west of the towns of Berkeley Heights, New Providence, and Summit.

HOURS: Dawn to dusk.

ENTRANCE FEE: None.

HANDICAP ACCESS: None.

PICNICKING: Some tables, no restroom.

BOATING: Allowed in the river, which is suitable for small boats. The best entry point is in Berkeley Heights, near the bridge over the

Passaic River Park.

river at Snyder Avenue. There is a small gravel parking lot and a path that goes down to the river.

FISHING: Permitted in the Passaic River.

For additional information:
Union County Department of Parks and Recreation
Administration Building
Elizabeth, NJ 07207
Telephone: (908) 527-4900

 # Rahway River Park

St. Georges Avenue ♦ *Rahway, Union County* ♦ *133 acres*

LOCATION: This linear park is located east of the Garden State Parkway, at exit 135, and west of exit 136. Access is also from Route 27, north of Rahway.

HOURS: The grounds are open from dawn to dusk. The pool is open from late June to September 1: on Monday and Wednesday, from 1:00 P.M. to 8:00 P.M.; on Tuesday, Thursday, and Friday, from 1:00 P.M. to 6:00 P.M.; and on Saturday, Sunday, and holidays, from 11:00 A.M. to 6:00 P.M.

ENTRANCE FEE: Fee charged for pool.

HANDICAP ACCESS: Tables at the picnic area are handicap accessible.

PICNICKING: Tables with grills, a playground, and a restroom.

FISHING: Permitted in the Rahway River.

SWIMMING: Swimming can be enjoyed in the Walter E. Ulrich Memorial Pool. For more information, call (732) 381-4045.

> **For additional information:**
> Union County Department of Parks and Recreation
> Administration Building
> Elizabeth, NJ 07207
> Telephone: 908 527-4900

 # Ramapo Mountain State Forest

Passaic and Bergen Counties • *4,200 acres*

LOCATION: Take I–287 to exit 57, and follow Skyline Drive to the parking lot on the left.

HOURS: Dawn to dusk.

ENTRANCE FEE: None.

HANDICAP ACCESS: Access to fishing.

DESCRIPTION: A rugged mountain forest preserve with rocky ridges and outcrops, streams, lakes, swamps, and scenic overlooks.

FISHING: Permitted in 120-acre Ramapo Lake (approximately three miles of shoreline), for bass and pickerel.

HIKING: Forty-two-mile network of primitive, marked trails.

MOUNTAIN BIKING: Permitted on all trails.

HORSEBACK RIDING: Permitted on all trails.

HUNTING: Permitted in designated areas of the park (442 acres), for deer, small game, turkey, and waterfowl.

> **For additional information:**
> c/o Ringwood State Park
> 1304 Sloatsburg Road
> Ringwood, NJ 07456–1799
> Telephone: (973) 962-7031

Ramapo Valley County Reservation

Ramapo Valley Road (Route 202) ◆ *Mahwah,*
Bergen County ◆ *2,145 acres*

LOCATION: Off Route 202 (Ramapo Valley Road), north of Oakland. The entrance to the park is on the west side of the road.

HOURS: Dawn to dusk.

ENTRANCE FEE: None.

HANDICAP ACCESS: Access to fishing area.

CAMPING: Ten sites located in the vicinity of the Ramapo River and Scarlet Oak Pond. Each site has a lean-to, table, and fire ring. All supplies must be walked in. A modern restroom with hot shower is nearby. Call (201) 825-1388 for permits.

PICNICKING: Scattered sites, with tables and fire pits.

BOATING: Walk-in access to the Ramapo River.

FISHING: Permitted in the Ramapo River, which is stocked with trout. Also permitted in Scarlet Oak Pond (22 acres), Macmillan Reservoir (12 acres), and Bear Swamp Lake (48 acres).

Ramapo Valley County Reservation.

HIKING: Fifteen miles of marked and unmarked trails. Map available.

WINTER ACTIVITIES: Cross-country skiing.

For additional information:
Bergen County Department of Parks
One Bergen County Plaza, 4th floor
Hackensack, NJ 07601–7076
Telephone: (201) 336-7275; Fax: (201) 336-7262

Richard W. Dekorte Park

Bergen County ◆ *110 acres*

LOCATION: From Route 17, proceed straight at the traffic signal to Polito Avenue, until Valley Brook Avenue. Turn east, and proceed 2 miles to the Environment Center entrance.

HOURS: The grounds are open from dawn to dusk. The Environment Center is open daily, from 9:00 A.M. to 5:00 P.M., and on Saturday and Sunday, from 10:00 A.M. to 3:00 P.M.

ENTRANCE FEE: None.

New Jersey Meadowlands Commission staff

Dekorte Park.

Dekorte Park.

HANDICAP ACCESS: Most of the trails are handicap accessible. The Meadowlands Environment Center building is easily accessible with ramps, and it has a wheelchair accessible restroom.

SPECIAL FEATURES

Meadowlands Environment Center—Interactive exhibits and displays of the Meadowlands environment, as well as a gift shop and restrooms. For more information, call (201) 460-8300.

PICNICKING: Tables, no grills. Restrooms are in the Environment Center.

HIKING: Five marked trails, totaling three and a half miles.

BIRDWATCHING: There are several bird blinds throughout the park.

For additional information:
1 Dekorte Park Place
Lyndhurst, NJ 07071
Telephone: (201) 460-1700

 Rifle Camp Park

Rifle Camp Road ◆ West Paterson, Passaic County ◆
153 acres

LOCATION: Take I–80 to exit 56A (Squirrelwood Road, West Paterson). Drive south on Squirrelwood Road for 0.4 miles, to its end at Rifle

Camp Road. Turn east, and go about 0.9 miles to the park entrance on the north side of the road, just past the fire station. The Nature Center is located about 1 mile from the entrance, at the last parking lot.

HOURS: The grounds are open from dawn to dusk. The Nature Center is open daily, from 9:00 A.M. to 4:00 P.M.

ENTRANCE FEE: No fee.

HANDICAP ACCESS: One of the picnic areas is handicap accessible.

SPECIAL FEATURES
John J. Crowley Nature Center—The center has an astronomical observatory that is open for public viewing. It also has the only seismograph on public display along the East Coast. For more information, call (973) 523-0024.

PICNICKING: Two picnic areas with grills, a playground, and a restroom.

HIKING: One marked trail, two miles in length, in addition to other unmarked nature and walking trails.

BIRDWATCHING: A blind is located near the Nature Center.

WINTER ACTIVITIES: Cross-country skiing and sledding.

> **For additional information:**
> *Passaic County Parks Department*
> *311 Pennsylvania Avenue*
> *Paterson, NJ 07503*
> *Telephone: (973) 881-4832*

 # Ringwood State Park

Passaic and Bergen Counties ◆ 5,173 acres

Ringwood Manor

DESCRIPTION: A national historic landmark, and the former estate of Abram S. Hewitt, America's foremost ironmaster. The main office is located here.

LOCATION: From Route 23, take Route 511 north, toward Ringwood.

HOURS: The grounds are open daily, from 8:00 A.M. to 8:00 P.M., year-round. The Manor is open for tours Wednesday through Sunday, from 10:00 A.M. to 3:00 P.M., year-round.

ENTRANCE FEE: Fee charged.

HANDICAP ACCESS: The first floor of the Manor and restrooms are handicap accessible.

PICNICKING: Tables, with grills, a playground, and restrooms.

FISHING: Permitted in Ringwood Brook, which is stocked with trout.

HIKING: Marked and unmarked trails.

Skyland Manor

DESCRIPTION: Built in the 1920s, this is the former summer residence of Clarence MacKenzie Lewis, a New York stockbroker and civil engineer.

LOCATION: From Route 23, take Route 511 north, toward Ringwood.

HOURS: The grounds are open daily, from 8:00 A.M. to 8:00 P.M., year-round. The Manor is open for tours on the first Sunday of each month, April through November, from 12:00 P.M. to 4:00 P.M.

ENTRANCE FEE: Fee charged.

HANDICAP ACCESS: The Manor is not handicap accessible. The Carriage House Visitors' Center and restrooms are.

SPECIAL FEATURES
State Botanical Garden—Ninety-six acres of plantings and formal gardens. Open year-round.

PICNICKING: Tables, with grills, a playground, and restrooms.

HIKING: Marked and unmarked trails.

MOUNTAIN BIKING: Permitted on multi-use trails.

HORSEBACK RIDING: Permitted on multi-use trails.

For more information, call the Skylands Association at (973) 962-7527.

Shepherd Lake

DESCRIPTION: A recreational center located on the border of New York and New Jersey.

LOCATION: From Route 23, take Route 511 north, toward Ringwood.

HOURS: Open daily, from 8:00 A.M. to 8:00 P.M., year-round.

ENTRANCE FEE: Fee charged.

HANDICAP ACCESS: The lodge/bathhouse is handicap accessible, as are ramps for fishing.

PICNICKING: Tables, with grills, a playground, and restrooms.

BOATING: At 74-acre Shepherd Lake marina. Boat rentals, live bait, and supplies are available at the boathouse. Trailer and car-top boat ramp. For more information, call (973) 962-6999.

SWIMMING: Shepherd Lake has a sand beach, changing rooms, a snack bar, first aid, restrooms, and public telephones. Changing rooms close at 6:30 P.M.

FISHING: Permitted in Shepherd Lake.

HIKING: Marked and unmarked trails.

TRAP AND SKEET SHOOTING: Concession open all year. For more information, call (973) 962-6377.

HUNTING: Permitted in designated areas of the park (3,637 acres), for deer, small game, turkey, and waterfowl.

WINTER ACTIVITIES: Cross-country skiing and snowmobiling.

For additional information:
1304 Sloatsburg Road
Ringwood, NJ 07456–799
Telephone: (973) 962-7031

 # Riverside County Park

River Road   ◆   North Arlington, Bergen County   ◆
110 acres

LOCATION: Off Route 507 (River Road), and south of Route 3.

HOURS: Dawn to dusk.

ENTRANCE FEE: None.

HANDICAP ACCESS: The playground is handicap accessible.

PICNICKING: Available, with a playground and restrooms.

HIKING: Paved walking paths.

For additional information:
Bergen County Department of Parks
One Bergen County Plaza, 4th floor
Hackensack, NJ 07601–7076
Telephone: (201) 336-7275; Fax: (201) 336-7262

Saddle River County Park

Bergen County ◆ 596 acres

DESCRIPTION: Situated alongside the Saddle River in Bergen County, this park is comprised of five recreation areas that are linked by a bicycle-pedestrian path.

Wild Duck Pond Area

East Ridgewood Avenue, Ridgewood

LOCATION: East of Paramus Road, and north of East Ridgewood Avenue.

HOURS: Dawn to dusk.

ENTRANCE FEE: None.

HANDICAP ACCESS: None.

PICNICKING: Facilities, with a playground nearby.

FISHING: Permitted in 4-acre pond.

WINTER ACTIVITIES: Ice skating.

Glen Rock Area

Alan Avenue, Glen Rock

LOCATION: West of Saddle River Road, and south of Grove Street.

HOURS: Dawn to dusk.

ENTRANCE FEE: None.

HANDICAP ACCESS: None.

PICNICKING: Facilities, with a playground nearby.

FISHING: Permitted in the pond.

WINTER ACTIVITIES: Ice skating.

Dunkerhook Area

Saddle River Road, Saddle Brook

LOCATION: West of Saddle River Road, and north of Fairlawn.

HOURS: Dawn to dusk.

ENTRANCE FEE: None.

HANDICAP ACCESS: None.

PICNICKING: Facilities, with a playground nearby.

FISHING: Permitted in the lake.

Otto C. Pehle Area

Saddle River Road, Saddle Brook

LOCATION: West of Saddle River Road, at Lewis Street.

HOURS: Dawn to dusk.

ENTRANCE FEE: None.

HANDICAP ACCESS: None.

PICNICKING: Facilities, with a playground nearby.

FISHING: Permitted in 8-acre lake.

Rochelle Park Area

Railroad Avenue, Rochelle Park

LOCATION: West of Route 17, and north of I–80.

HOURS: Dawn to dusk.

ENTRANCE FEE: None.

HANDICAP ACCESS: None.

PICNICKING: Facilities, with a playground nearby.

WINTER ACTIVITIES: Ice skating.

For additional information:
Bergen County Department of Parks
One Bergen County Plaza, 4th floor
Hackensack, NJ 07601–7076
Telephone: (201) 336-7275; Fax: (201) 336-7262

Samuel Nelkin County Park

Rose Street ◆ *Wallington, Bergen County* ◆ *23 acres*

LOCATION: From Route 17, in the vicinity of Carlstadt, take Paterson Avenue west to Rose Street.

HOURS: Dawn to dusk.

ENTRANCE FEE: None.

HANDICAP ACCESS: None.

FISHING: Permitted in the pond.

PICNICKING: Tables, with a playground.

WINTER ACTIVITIES: Ice skating and sledding.

For additional information:
Bergen County Department of Parks
One Bergen County Plaza, 4th floor
Hackensack, NJ 07601–7076
Telephone: (201) 336-7275; Fax: (201) 336-7262

 # Sawmill Creek
Wildlife Management Area

Bergen and Hudson Counties ◆ *727 acres*

LOCATION: Situated between the east and west spurs of the New Jersey Turnpike, near exit 15W.

HOURS: Dawn to dusk.

ENTRANCE FEE: None.

HANDICAP ACCESS: None.

FISHING: Permitted in the Hackensack River.

CRABBING: Permitted in the Hackensack River.

HUNTING: For waterfowl.

For additional information:
New Jersey Division of Fish and Wildlife
Trenton Office
501 E. State Street, P.O. Box 400
Trenton, NJ 08625–0400
Telephone: (609) 984-0547

South Mountain Reservation

Northfield Road and South Orange Avenue ✦
Maplewood, Millburn, and West Orange ✦ *Essex County* ✦
2,048 acres

LOCATION: Access is best from either South Orange Avenue, or North-field Road.

HOURS: The grounds are open from dawn to dusk. Turtle Back Zoo is open year-round, Monday through Saturday, from 10:00 A.M. to 4:30 P.M., and on Sunday, from 11:00 A.M. to 5:30 P.M.

ENTRANCE FEE: None for the park. There is an entrance fee for the zoo.

HANDICAP ACCESS: Turtle Back Zoo is handicap accessible.

SPECIAL FEATURES

Turtle Back Zoo—This is an 18-acre zoo. Located at 560 Northfield Avenue, West Orange, NJ 07052. For more information, call (973) 731-5800.

PICNICKING: A number of different areas have tables and grills, most with restrooms.

Turtle Back Zoo.

FISHING: Permitted in 4-acre Diamond Mill Pond, which is stocked with trout. It is also permitted in the Rahway River, which runs through the park.

HIKING: Six marked trails, totaling more than nineteen miles.

HORSEBACK RIDING: Twenty-seven miles of carriage roads open to horseback riding.

WINTER ACTIVITIES: Cross-country skiing.

For additional information:
Essex County Department of Parks, Recreation & Cultural Affairs
115 Clifton Avenue
Newark, NJ 07104
Telephone: (973) 268-3500

Stephen R. Gregg Park

Kennedy Boulevard and 43rd Street ◆ Bayonne, Hudson County ◆ 98 acres

LOCATION: Off Route 501 (J.F. Kennedy Boulevard), south of I–78.

HOURS: Dawn to dusk.

ENTRANCE FEE: None.

HANDICAP ACCESS: The fishing area is handicap accessible.

PICNICKING: Picnic area with a playground and restrooms.

FISHING: Permitted from the pier in Newark bay.

CRABBING: Permitted from the pier.

For additional information:
Hudson County Parks and Recreation
Administration Building, Lincoln Park
Jersey City, NJ 07304
Telephone: (201) 915-1386; Fax: (201) 915-1385

Tenafly Nature Center

Tenafly, Bergen County ◆ 52 acres

LOCATION: East of Route 501, in Tenafly.

HOURS: The grounds are open from dawn to dusk. The Visitor Center is open Tuesday to Saturday, from 9:00 A.M. to 5 P.M.; on Sunday, from 10:00 A.M. to 5 P.M.; and on Monday, from 1:00 P.M. to 5:00 P.M. When the visitor parking lot is closed, parking is available on Hudson Avenue.

ENTRANCE FEE: None.

HANDICAP ACCESS: The new education pavilion at the Visitor Center and the composting restroom are handicap accessible.

SPECIAL FEATURES
John A. Redfield Building—Small natural history museum, live animal displays, gift shop, and library.

HIKING: More than seven miles of marked trails, mostly within the adjacent Lost Brook Preserve, which is largely undeveloped. Trail map available.

WINTER ACTIVITIES: Cross-country skiing and ice skating.

For additional information:
313 Hudson Avenue
Tenafly, NJ 07670
Telephone: (201) 568-6093; Fax: (201) 569-2266;
Website: www.tenaflynaturecenter.org

 Van Saun County Park

Forest and Continental Avenues ◆ *Bergen County* ◆
140 acres

LOCATION: From Route 4, east of Route 17, turn north onto Forest Avenue. Entrances also on Continental Avenue and Howland Avenue.

HOURS: The grounds are open from dawn to dusk. The zoo is open daily, from 10:00 A.M. to 4:30 P.M.

ENTRANCE FEE: An entrance fee is charged for the zoo on weekends and holidays, from May through October.

HANDICAP ACCESS: The zoo can be enjoyed by handicapped people, and the playground nearest the zoo can also be safely enjoyed by children who are disabled.

SPECIAL FEATURES
Pony Riding concession—For small children; ponies are led in a circle. Open from April through November. For more information, call (201) 599-9800.

Van Saun Park Zoo—This well-maintained zoo is accredited by the American Association of Zoological Parks and Aquariums. During the colder months, many of the exhibits are closed. Open year-round. For more information, call (201) 262-3771.

Miniature Train—A replica of an 1866 locomotive pulls canopied coaches in a loop around the zoo, passing by an 1860s farmyard scene and through a tunnel. Open from April through October. For more information, call (201) 262-3771, ext. 22.

PICNICKING: Several different areas, with playgrounds and restrooms nearby.

FISHING: Permitted in 4-acre Walden Pond.

WINTER ACTIVITIES: Ice skating.

> **For additional information:**
> Bergen County Department of Parks
> One Bergen County Plaza, 4th floor
> Hackensack, NJ 07601–7076
> Telephone: (201) 336-7275; Fax: (201) 336-7262

Verona Park

Bloomfield Avenue ◆ Verona, Essex County ◆ 54 acres

LOCATION: South of Route 506 (Bloomfield Avenue), in Verona, and east of Lakeside Avenue.

HOURS: The grounds are open from dawn to dusk; the boathouse is open daily, from 9:00 A.M. to 7:30 P.M.

ENTRANCE FEE: None.

HANDICAP ACCESS: None.

BOATING: Allowed in the 13-acre lake. The boathouse rents rowboats and paddle boats. For more information, call (973) 239-2774.

FISHING: Permitted in the lake.

HIKING: Three miles of walking trails.

> **For additional information:**
> Essex County Department of Parks, Recreation & Cultural Affairs
> 115 Clifton Avenue
> Newark, NJ 07104
> Telephone: (973) 268-3500

Wanaque Wildlife Management Area

East Shore Road ◆ Passaic County ◆ 2,319 acres

LOCATION: East of Greenwood Lake. Take Route 511, west of Ringwood, to East Shore Road, which runs through the tract.

HOURS: Dawn to dusk.

ENTRANCE FEE: None.

HANDICAP ACCESS: None.

BOATING: A launch site for both car-top and trailer boats is available at the north end of Green Turtle Pond. Access is from Awosting Road, off Route 511, west of the turnoff for East Shore Road.

FISHING: Permitted in 40-acre Green Turtle Pond for largemouth bass and chain pickerel, and in the Wanaque River for trout.

HIKING: Informal trails.

MOUNTAIN BIKING: Allowed on existing trails and secondary roads from March 1 to April 15, and from June 1 to September 15, as well as on all Sundays throughout the year.

HUNTING: For deer, small game, turkey, and waterfowl.

WINTER ACTIVITIES: Cross-country skiing on all trails on Sunday.

Greg Johnson

Wanaque Wildlife Management Area.

For additional information:
New Jersey Division of Fish and Wildlife
Trenton Office
501 E. State Street, P.O. Box 400
Trenton, NJ 08625–0400
Telephone: (609) 984-0547

 # Warinanco Park

St. Georges Avenue ◆ Roselle, Union County ◆
204 acres

LOCATION: Access from St. Georges Avenue (Route 27) in Roselle, just west of Elizabeth.

HOURS: Dawn to dusk.

ENTRANCE FEE: None.

HANDICAP ACCESS: Picnic tables and the fishing area are handicap accessible.

SPECIAL FEATURES

Henry S. Chatfield Memorial Garden—Twenty-one garden beds have more than 14,000 tulips. The tulips are usually in bloom during the last two weeks of April and into early May. Afterwards the garden is planted with annuals.

PICNICKING: Picnic area with a playground. Restrooms are at the skating center, which is open all year.

BOATING: Allowed in 8-acre lake. Paddle boats can be rented at the boathouse from April through September, on weekdays, from 1:00 P.M. to 6:30 P.M., and on weekends, from 11:00 A.M. to 6:30 P.M. For more information, call (908) 298-7845.

FISHING: Permitted in the lake.

WINTER ACTIVITIES: Ice skating. Call the skating center at (908) 298-7849.

For additional information:
Union County Department of Parks and Recreation
Administration Building
Elizabeth, NJ 07207
Telephone: (908) 527-4900

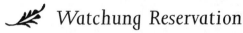

Watchung Reservation

Boroughs of New Providence and Mountainside,
Scotch Plains Township ◆ *Union County* ◆ *2,002 acres*

LOCATION: Located between Routes 78 and 22, north of Scotch Plains.

HOURS: The grounds are open from dawn to dusk. The Trailside Nature and Science Center includes the museum and Visitor Center. The museum is open daily, April through mid-November, from 1:00 P.M. to 5:00 P.M., and during winter school vacations. At other times of the year, it is open only on weekends. The Visitor Center is open daily, from 1:00 P.M. to 5:00 P.M.

ENTRANCE FEE: None.

HANDICAP ACCESS: The picnic area has handicap-accessible tables.

SPECIAL FEATURES

Watchung Stable—Located at 1160 Summit Lane, Mountainside, NJ 07092. Provides children and adults with the opportunity to learn to ride. Offers guided trail rides. For more information, call (908) 789-3665.

Deserted Village of Feltville—Consists of ten buildings dating from the mid-1800s. Tours are offered periodically.

Trailside Nature & Science Center—Consists of a visitor's center, a museum, and a planetarium.

Visitor Center—Permanent and changing exhibits, a gift shop, a bird-feeding station, a scent garden and a fern garden, park information and maps, beverage machines, and restrooms.

Museum—Exhibits, a discovery room for young children, and a butterfly garden.

Planetarium—Offers public shows, and has a gift shop.

PICNICKING: Several picnic areas are scattered throughout the park, one with a playground. All have water and restrooms nearby.

BOATING: Permitted in Surprise Lake. Car-top access for nonmotorized boats only.

FISHING: Permitted in 3-acre Seeley's Pond, 25-acre Lake Surprise, and Blue Brook. All three are stocked with trout.

HIKING: The park offers more than forty miles of unmarked trails, and thirteen miles of marked trails. A trail map is available.

HORSEBACK RIDING: There are twenty-six miles of bridle trails.

WINTER ACTIVITIES: Cross-country skiing.

For additional information:

Trailside Nature & Science Center
452 New Providence Road
Mountainside, NJ 07092
Telephone: (908) 789-3670
    or
Union County Department of Parks and Recreation
Administration Building
Elizabeth, NJ 07207
Telephone: (908) 527-4900

 # Weequahic County Park

Elizabeth Avenue   ◆   Newark, Essex County   ◆   311 acres

LOCATION: West of Route 27 (Frelinghuysen Avenue), and south of Route 22.

HOURS: Dawn to dusk.

Greg Johnson

Weequahic Park.

ENTRANCE FEE: None.

HANDICAP ACCESS: None.

PICNICKING: Picnic area overlooking the lake.

FISHING: Permitted in the 80-acre lake.

For additional information:

Weequahic Park Association
Telephone: (973) 643-7850
  or
Essex County Department of Parks, Recreation & Cultural Affairs
115 Clifton Avenue
Newark, NJ 07104
Telephone: (973) 268-3500

 # Weis Ecology Center

Ringwood, Passaic County • 160 *acres*

LOCATION: From Route 511, north of the town of Wanaque, turn west onto Westbrook Road, crossing Wanaque Reservoir. Bear left at the fork, and continue to Snake Den Road.

HOURS: The grounds are open from dawn to dusk; the office is open Wednesday through Sunday, from 8:30 A.M. to 4:30 P.M. Restrooms are locked at 4:30 P.M., October 15 through April 15.

ENTRANCE FEE: None.

HANDICAP ACCESS: None.

CABINS: Thirty primitive cabins each sleep four. The season runs from April 1 through October 31. Cabins have electricity (enough for a radio or lamp), but no running water or inside toilets. Payment includes use of the grounds. Bathroom and shower facilities are nearby.

CAMPING: Ten wooded sites with portable toilets. Payment includes use of the grounds.

HIKING: One marked trail. The center is adjacent to Norvin Green State Forest, allowing access to hiking at this location.

For additional information:

150 Snake Den Road
Ringwood, NJ 07456
Telephone: (973) 835-2160;
Website: www.njaudubon.org/Centers/Weis

West Essex County Park

Livingston, Roseland, and West Caldwell • Essex County •
1,360 acres

LOCATION: This linear park stretches along six miles of the Passaic River, starting at Bloomfield Avenue in Fairfield, and ending just beyond South Orange Avenue in Livingston.

HOURS: Dawn to dusk.

ENTRANCE FEE: None.

HANDICAP ACCESS: None.

BOATING: A canoe launch giving access to the Passaic River is located near Pine Brook Bridge.

FISHING: Permitted in the Passaic River.

HIKING: Informal trails.

For additional information:
Essex County Department of Parks, Recreation & Cultural Affairs
115 Clifton Avenue
Newark, NJ 07104
Telephone: (973) 268-3500

 # Wood Dale County Park

Prospect Avenue • Woodcliff Lake, Bergen County •
117 acres

LOCATION: Take Kinderkamack Road to Prospect Avenue.

HOURS: Dawn to dusk.

ENTRANCE FEE: None.

HANDICAP ACCESS: None.

FISHING: Permitted in the 2-acre pond.

PICNICKING: Tables, a playground, and a restroom.

WINTER ACTIVITIES: Ice skating.

For additional information:
Bergen County Department of Parks
One Bergen County Plaza, 4th floor
Hackensack, NJ 07601–7076
Telephone: (201) 336-7275; Fax: (201) 336-7262

Region Three

Hunterdon, Mercer, Middlesex, & Somerset Counties

Washington Crossing State Park.

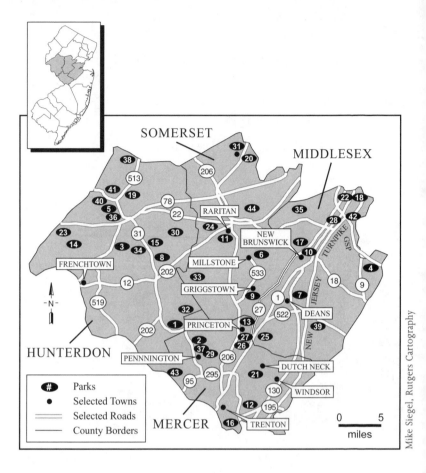

SOMERSET

MIDDLESEX

HUNTERDON

MERCER

FRENCHTOWN

RARITAN

NEW BRUNSWICK

MILLSTONE

GRIGGSTOWN

PRINCETON

PENNINGTON

DEANS

DUTCH NECK

WINDSOR

TRENTON

NEW JERSEY TURNPIKE

GSP

-N-

● Parks
● Selected Towns
▦ Selected Roads
— County Borders

0   5
miles

Mike Siegel, Rutgers Cartography

1   Amwell Lake Wildlife Management Area
2   Baldwin Lake Wildlife Management Area
3   Capoolong Creek Wildlife Management Area
4   Cheesequake State Park
5   Clinton Wildlife Management Area
6   Colonial Park
7   Davidson's Mill Pond Park
8   Deer Path Park
9   Delaware and Raritan Canal State Park
10 Donaldson Park
11 Duke Island Park
12 Hamilton Veterans Park
13 Herrontown Woods
14 Hoffman Park
15 Hunterdon County Arboretum
16 John A. Roebling Park
17 Johnson Park
18 Joseph Medwick Park
19 Ken Lockwood Gorge Wildlife Management Area
20 Lord Stirling Park
21 Mercer County Park
22 Merrill Park
23 Musconetcong River Reservation
24 North Branch Park
25 Plainsboro Preserve
26 Princeton Battlefield State Park
27 Princeton Institute Woods
28 Roosevelt Park
29 Rosedale Park
30 Round Valley Recreation Area
31 Scherman-Hoffman Sanctuaries
32 Sourland Mountain Nature Preserve
33 Sourland Mountain Preserve
34 South Branch Reservation
35 Spring Lake Park
36 Spruce Run Recreation Area
37 Stony Brook–Millstone Watershed Association Nature Preserve
38 Teetertown Ravine Nature Preserve
39 Thompson Park
40 Union Furnace Nature Preserve
41 Voorhees State Park
42 Warren Park
43 Washington Crossing State Park
44 Washington Valley Park

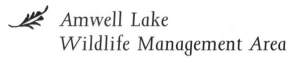 Amwell Lake
Wildlife Management Area

Route 31, Hunterdon County ◆ 22 acres

LOCATION: Off Route 31, east of Linvale. The access road is about 0.25 miles north of the Harbourton turnoff.

HOURS: Dawn to dusk.

ENTRANCE FEE: None.

HANDICAP ACCESS: None.

BOATING: Small boats, no gas motors.

FISHING: Shoreline and boat fishing is permitted. The 10-acre lake is stocked with rainbow and brown trout.

For additional information:
New Jersey Division of Fish and Wildlife
Trenton Office
501 E. State Street, P.O. Box 400
Trenton, NJ 08625–0400
Telephone: (609) 984-0547

Amwell Lake Wildlife Management Area.

Baldwin Lake
Wildlife Management Area

Mercer County • *47 acres*

LOCATION: North of Pennington, on Route 31. Turn at the county road, toward Mt. Rose Road. The wildlife management area is about 0.25 miles north of the intersection at Mt. Rose Road.

HOURS: Dawn to dusk.

ENTRANCE FEE: None.

HANDICAP ACCESS: None.

FISHING: Shoreline fishing is permitted, for bass and sunfish.

For additional information:
New Jersey Division of Fish and Wildlife
Trenton Office
501 E. State Street, P.O. Box 400
Trenton, NJ 08625–0400
Telephone: (609) 984-0547

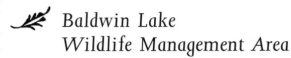 # Capoolong Creek
Wildlife Management Area

Pittstown, Kingtown, and Sidney • *Hunterdon County* • *63 acres*

LOCATION: Formerly the Pittstown-Landsdown abandoned Lehigh Valley railroad right-of-way. The tract is located off Route 513, from Pittstown to Landsdown. Cars can be parked at two spots, either along Kingtown-Sidney Road or at the old railroad station in Pittstown. Kingtown-Sidney Road can be accessed from Route 617 (Cherryvill Road), south of Sidney.

HOURS: Dawn to dusk.

ENTRANCE FEE: None.

HANDICAP ACCESS: None.

DESCRIPTION: Capoolong Creek is one of the few streams in New Jersey that supports a natural trout population.

FISHING: The area is stocked with brook, brown, and rainbow trout, in addition to the natural trout population. Smallmouth bass and rock bass are also present.

HIKING: Informal trails.

WINTER ACTIVITIES: Cross-country skiing on all trails on Sunday.

For additional information:
New Jersey Division of Fish and Wildlife
Trenton Office
501 E. State Street, P.O. Box 400
Trenton, NJ 08625–0400
Telephone: (609) 984-0547

Charles H. Rogers Wildlife Refuge
(see Princeton Institute Woods)

Cheesequake State Park
Old Bridge, Middlesex County • 1,420 acres

LOCATION: Take the Garden State Parkway to exit 120. Follow signs.

HOURS: The grounds are open from 8:00 A.M. to dusk. The Interpretive Center is open Wednesday through Sunday, from 8:00 A.M. to 4:00 P.M., September through May; and June through August, seven days a week.

ENTRANCE FEE: Fee charged from Memorial Day weekend to Labor Day.

HANDICAP ACCESS: Campsite reserved for handicapped, and picnic area is handicap accessible.

DESCRIPTION: Only thirty miles from New York City, and with easy access from the Garden State Parkway, Cheesequake is accessible to a large number of people.

SPECIAL FEATURES

Interpretive Center—Exhibits at the Interpretive Center focus on the diversity of ecosystems located within the park. There are live exhibits of fish and turtles, along with weekly interpretive programming. For more information, call (732) 566-3208.

CAMPING: Fifty-three family campsites for tents and trailers, each with a picnic table and fire ring. The camping area has modern restrooms, a coin-operated laundry, a dumping station for trailers, and seasonal hot showers. The area is open from April 1 through October 31. Reservations are recommended.

Cheesequake State Park.

PICNICKING: Six picnic areas are situated throughout the park and are equipped with tables and grills or stone fireplaces. A playground is nearby.

BOATING: Car-top boat launching in 10-acre Hooks Creek Lake is permitted from the day after Labor Day through the day before Memorial Day weekend. Electric motors only.

FISHING: Permitted in the lake and creek.

CRABBING: Permitted in Hooks Creek during late summer and early fall. A crabbing bridge is located near the bathing beach.

SWIMMING: The lifeguard-supervised beach is open during the summer. Restrooms and changing rooms are located at the beach area, as are first aid and a concession stand for refreshments and beach supplies.

HIKING: Five marked trails, the longest of which is three and a half miles. Trail guides are available for two of the trails.

MOUNTAIN BIKING: Permitted on designated trails and sand roads.

WINTER ACTIVITIES: Cross-country skiing, ice skating, and sledding.

For additional information:
300 Gordon Road
Matawan, NJ 07747
Telephone: (732) 566-2161;
Website: www.cheesequakestatepark.com

Clinton Wildlife Management Area

Van Syckels Road, Hunterdon County ◆ *1,586 acres*

LOCATION: Adjacent to Spruce Run Reservoir, east of Route 31, and north of Route 78.

HOURS: Dawn to dusk.

ENTRANCE FEE: None.

HANDICAP ACCESS: None.

BOATING: Motorboats are limited to a maximum of ten horsepower and twenty-five feet. A boat launch is located off Van Syckels Road, north of the entrance to the recreation area.

FISHING: Permitted in the 5-acre pond.

HIKING: Informal trails.

MOUNTAIN BIKING: Allowed on existing trails and secondary roads from March 1 to April 15, and from June 1 to September 15, as well as on all Sundays throughout the year.

HUNTING: For deer, small game, turkey, and waterfowl.

WINTER ACTIVITIES: Cross-country skiing on all trails on Sunday.

For additional information:
New Jersey Division of Fish and Wildlife
Trenton Office
501 E. State Street, P.O. Box 400
Trenton, NJ 08625–0400
Telephone: (609) 984-0547

Colonial Park

Metlars Road ◆ *Franklin Township, Somerset County* ◆ *462 acres*

LOCATION: Take Route 514 (Amwell Road), east of Route 533, to Metlars Road.

Colonial Park.

HOURS: The grounds and park office are open from dawn to dusk. Paddle Boat rental and Miniature Golf are open daily, Memorial Day weekend through Labor Day, from 10:00 A.M. to 8:00 P.M.; and in April, May, September, and October, on weekends, from 12:00 P.M. to 8:00 P.M.

ENTRANCE FEE: None.

HANDICAP ACCESS: The walking trail, rose garden, and restrooms are handicap accessible.

SPECIAL FEATURES

The Rudolph van der Goot Rose Garden—More than four thousand roses. Located in the western part of the park.

MINIATURE GOLF: Located next to the paddle boats. Fee charged for use.

PICNICKING: There are two main picnic groves, each with tables, grills, and a playground nearby. Restrooms are open from April 15 through November 15.

FISHING: Permitted in 3-acre Metlars Pond, in the canal, and in the Millstone River.

Colonial Park Rose Garden in Somerset County.

BOATING: Paddle boats can be rented at 6-acre Powder Mill Pond. For more information, call (732) 873-8585. A canoe launch is available for access to the Delaware and Raritan canal.

HIKING: Several marked trails, in addition to a nature trail, are located across the street from Powder Mill Pond.

MOUNTAIN BIKING: Permitted on some trails.

HORSEBACK RIDING: Permitted on the bridle trail.

WINTER ACTIVITIES: Cross-country skiing, and ice skating on the pond.

For additional information:

Colonial Park Ranger Office
Telephone: (732) 873-2695

Somerset County Park Commission
355 Milltown Road, P.O. Box 5327
Bridgewater, NJ 08876
Telephone: (908) 722-1200; Fax: (908) 722-6592

Davidson's Mill Pond Park

Riva *Avenue* ◆ South Brunswick, Middlesex County ◆
482 *acres*

LOCATION: Take Route 130 in South Brunswick to Davidson's Mill Road, and go south on Riva Avenue.

HOURS: Dawn to dusk.

ENTRANCE FEE: None.

HANDICAP ACCESS: None.

PICNICKING: Some tables, with seasonal toilets.

BOATING: Allowed in the 10-acre lake. A boat ramp is available for trailer and car-top boats.

FISHING: Permitted in the lake and in two ponds.

HIKING: Informal trails.

WINTER ACTIVITIES: Cross-country skiing.

For additional information:
Middlesex County Department of Parks and Recreation
P.O. Box 661
New Brunswick, NJ 08903
Telephone: (732) 745-3900

Davidson's Mill Pond Park.

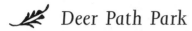 Deer Path Park

West Woodschurch Road ◆ *Hunterdon County* ◆ *159 acres*

LOCATION: Located about 3 miles south of the Hunterdon County Arboretum. From Route 31, turn west onto West Woodschurch Road.

HOURS: Dawn to dusk.

ENTRANCE FEE: None.

HANDICAP ACCESS: The picnic area is handicap accessible.

PICNICKING: Picnic areas, with a playground and restrooms located nearby.

FISHING: Permitted in the 3-acre pond; catch and release.

HIKING: Two loop trails, one long and one short. Parts of the trail may be seasonally wet.

HORSEBACK RIDING: Permitted on all trails.

WINTER ACTIVITIES: Cross-country skiing.

Horses on Round Mountain, Deer Path Park.

Doug Kiovsky

Deer Path Park Playground.

Round Mountain Section

Readington Township, Hunterdon County ◆ *236 acres*

LOCATION: East of route 31, and south of Route 629, on West Woods-church Road. Parking and restrooms at Deer Path Park, which is across the street.

HOURS: Dawn to dusk.

ENTRANCE FEE: None.

HANDICAP ACCESS: None.

HIKING: Several marked trails, including a self-guided nature trail.

MOUNTAIN BIKING: Permitted on trails.

HORSEBACK RIDING: Permitted on trails.

HUNTING: For deer, in designated areas.

WINTER ACTIVITIES: Cross-country skiing.

Note: Visitors to this park are requested to wear blaze orange during hunting season, or to confine their visits to Sunday.

For Additional information:
Hunterdon County Department of Parks and Recreation
P.O. Box 2900
Flemington, NJ 08822–2900
Telephone: (908) 782-1158; Fax: (908) 806-4057

 # Delaware and Raritan Canal State Park

Canal Road, Somerset ◆ *4,456 acres*

LOCATION: Parking is available in designated parking lots along the canal towpath. The main canal runs from Trenton to New Brunswick, with a break at the Route 1 crossing. It flows along the Millstone and Raritan Rivers, and is paralleled by the original towpath. The park office is located at Blackwells Mills. To get to it, take Route 206 to Hillsborough, to Route 514 east (Amwell Road). Then turn right onto Route 533 south (Millstone River Road). Travel for 2.1 miles, and turn left, across the bridge, onto Blackwells Mills Road and across Canal Bridge. Turn right on Canal Road, and it is the second structure on the left.

Delaware and Raritan Canal State Park.

HOURS: Dawn to dusk.

ENTRANCE FEE: None.

HANDICAP ACCESS: None.

DESCRIPTION: Opened in 1834, the canal served for a century as an important link between Trenton and New Brunswick, with the overall purpose of providing a safe and short waterway between Philadelphia (via the Delaware River) and New York (via the Raritan River). The canal ceased operation in 1933. It was taken over by the state and used as a source of water for farms, industry, and homes. The park was established in 1974. It consists of the feeder and main canals. The feeder canal flows along the Delaware River, from Trenton north to Frenchtown, and is paralleled by a recycled railroad right-of-way called the Multi-Use Trail (MUT). The main canal flows along the Millstone and Raritan Rivers, and is paralleled by the original towpath.

SPECIAL FEATURES

Six Mile Run Reservoir—This area offers 3,037 acres of land, open for hiking, biking, horseback riding, and birdwatching. More than six miles of marked trails. Map available at park office.

PICNICKING: Established sites can be found in Washington Crossing State, Griggstown, Blackwells Mills (about three miles north of Griggstown) and the South Bound Brook lock. There are tables and grills, and seasonal portable toilets are open from April through November.

BOATING: The entire park is open to canoeing or row boating (locks must be forded) except for the one-and-one-quarter-mile section that flows under Route 1. Canoes can be rented at several locations. Gasoline motors are not permitted.

FISHING: The entire length of the park is open to fishing. Year-round populations include largemouth bass, bluegill, pumpkinseed, catfish, perch, and pickerel. The Princeton section of the canal is stocked yearly with trout.

HIKING: Approximately sixty-four miles of trails are available along the feeder and main canals. At the Griggstown Canal lock, a parking area can be found at the beginning of the Silver Maple Nature Trail, a one-mile trail that runs along the Millstone River.

MOUNTAIN BIKING: Permitted on the towpath and the MUT.

HORSEBACK RIDING: Permitted on the entire length of the towpath, but not on the MUT.

HUNTING: Permitted in designated areas (800 acres) of Six Mile Run Reservoir site, for deer bow-hunting.

WINTER ACTIVITIES: Cross-country skiing.

Bull's Island Recreation Area

Stockton • 80 acres

LOCATION: Bull's Island Recreation Area can be reached by taking I–287 or Route 22 to the intersection with Route 202 in Somerville. Follow Route 202 south for 26 miles, to the exit for Route 29 north. Go north on Route 29 for about 6 miles. The entrance is on the left.

HOURS: Dawn to dusk.

ENTRANCE FEE: None.

HANDICAP ACCESS: None.

CAMPING: Sixty-nine tent and trailer sites are available at Bull's Island from April 1 through October 31. Facilities include flush toilets, hot showers, a dumping station, a laundry, and outside drinking water. Each site has a table and fire ring. No electric or water hookups.

PICNICKING: Tables and grills. Restroom nearby.

BOATING: Boat ramp gives access to the Delaware River.

FISHING: Permitted in the Delaware River and in the canal.

> **For additional information:**
>
> *Delaware & Raritan Canal State Park*
> 643 Canal Road
> Somerset, NJ 08873
> Telephone: (732) 873-3050; Website: www.dandrcanal.com
>
> *Bull's Island Recreation Area*
> 2185 Daniel Bray Highway
> Stockton, NJ 08559
> Telephone: (609) 397-2949

 # Donaldson Park

South Second Avenue ◆ *Highland Park, Middlesex County* ◆ *90 acres*

LOCATION: Take Route 27 into Highland Park, and turn south onto South Second Avenue. After four blocks, it leads into the park.

HOURS: Dawn to dusk

ENTRANCE FEE: None.

HANDICAP ACCESS: The restrooms are handicap accessible.

DESCRIPTION: This is the only park in the Middlesex County system with a boat ramp for large boats. If you've been wondering how to get your boat onto the Raritan River, here it is.

PICNICKING: There are four established picnic groves, all lightly wooded. Most have playgrounds and nearby restrooms.

BOATING: Boat ramp for trailer and car-top boats gives access to the Raritan River.

FISHING: Permitted in the pond near picnic grove 4, and in the Raritan River.

WINTER ACTIVITIES: Ice skating.

For additional information:
Middlesex County Department of Parks and Recreation
P.O. Box 661
New Brunswick, NJ 08903
Telephone: (732) 745-3900

 # Duke Island Park

Old York Road (Route 567) ◆ Bridgewater Township,
Somerset County ◆ 332 acres

LOCATION: Take Route 206, and turn west onto Old York Road (Route 567). Pass the town of Raritan. The park is on the south side of the road.

HOURS: The grounds are open from dawn to dusk. The Visitor Center is open from 9:00 A.M. to 9:00 P.M. on weekends, and from 1:00 P.M. to 9:00 P.M. on weekdays. Restrooms (located outside the Visitor Center) are open from 8:00 A.M. to 9:00 P.M.

ENTRANCE FEE: None.

HANDICAP ACCESS: One of the picnic groves is fully accessible, as is the picnic area playground.

DESCRIPTION: A nicely kept park with varied activities for the whole family.

SPECIAL FEATURES

Visitor Center—Wildlife exhibits and park information. Restrooms and a telephone are located outside the center. For more information, call (908) 722-7779.

PICNICKING: Areas are scattered throughout the park. Tables, with grills, are near large open fields, a playground, and the Raritan River, with a restroom nearby.

BOATING: Allowed on the north branch of the Raritan River. No boat launch is available.

FISHING: Permitted in the Raritan River and in the duck pond at the eastern end of the park.

HIKING: Marked trails.

WINTER ACTIVITIES: Cross-country skiing and ice skating.

For additional information:
Somerset County Park Commission
P.O. Box 5327
North Branch, NJ 08876
Telephone: (908) 722-1200; Fax: (908) 722-6592

Hamilton Veterans Park

Klockner Road • *Hamilton Township, Mercer County* •
300 acres

LOCATION: Exit I–95 at 3B, heading north. Continue straight off the ramp, and the eastern entrance to the park will be on the west side of the road. For the northern entrance, continue to the first intersection, and turn left on Klockner Road. The entrance to the park will be on the left.

HOURS: Dawn to dusk.

ENTRANCE FEE: None.

HANDICAP ACCESS: The picnic area is handicap accessible.

DESCRIPTION: This park stands out for its well-maintained appearance and its particularly large playground area with equipment appropriate for all ages.

PICNICKING: Tables with grills adjacent to a large playground. Some tables are placed along a stream that runs near the area.

BOATING: Small boats permitted without motors.

FISHING: Permitted in the lake.

HIKING: Trails throughout the park.

For additional information:
Hamilton Division of Recreation
320 Scully Avenue
Hamilton, NJ 08610
Telephone: (609) 890-3684

Herrontown Woods

Herrontown Road • *Princeton, Mercer County* • *142 acres*

LOCATION: Travel north on Nassau Street (Route 27). Continue 0.4 miles, past Harrison Street, to Snowden Lane. Turn left onto Snowden Lane, and travel 1.5 miles to driveway of Herrontown Woods.

Herrontown Woods.

HOURS: Dawn to dusk.

ENTRANCE FEE: None.

HANDICAP ACCESS: None.

HIKING: Three and a half miles of trails. A map can be found at the entrance to the trail.

> **For additional information:**
> *Mercer County Park Commission*
> *P.O. Box 8068*
> *Trenton, NJ 08560*
> *Telephone: (609) 989-6530*

Hoffman Park

Union Township, Hunterdon County ◆ *354 acres*

LOCATION: West of Clinton, and just south of I–78. Take I–78 west to exit 11. Follow the circle around to the left, and cross over I–78, following the signs for Pattenburg. Immediately after crossing I–78, turn left at the light. Proceed to the remains of an old church, and veer right onto Baptist Church Road. Proceed on Baptist Church Road under a railroad bridge, and shortly thereafter turn left into the park entrance, which is marked by a large brown sign.

HOURS: Open from 9:00 A.M. to dusk.

ENTRANCE FEE: None.

HANDICAP ACCESS: None.

FISHING: Permitted in five ponds, for bass and sunfish.

HIKING: Several trails, including old gravel roads. Trail map available.

MOUNTAIN BIKING: Permitted on all trails.

HUNTING: Limited hunting for deer.

WINTER ACTIVITIES: Cross-country skiing.

> **For additional information:**
> Hunterdon County Department of Parks and Recreation
> P.O. Box 2900
> Flemington, NJ 08822–2900
> Telephone: (908) 782-1158; Fax: (908) 806-4057

Hunterdon County Arboretum

Route 31 ◆ Hunterdon County ◆ 105 acres

LOCATION: On the east side of Route 31, approximately halfway between Clinton and Flemington.

HOURS: The grounds are open from dawn to dusk. The office is open weekdays from 8:30 A.M. to 4:30 P.M.; and on Saturday from 8:30 A.M. to 12:30 P.M.

ENTRANCE FEE: None.

HANDICAP ACCESS: One of the nature trails is handicap accessible.

DESCRIPTION: The gardens are attractive, and the grounds are pleasant. This is the headquarters for the Hunterdon County Park System, which can provide additional information about other parks in the system.

PICNICKING: Tables are available, no grills. Restrooms are in the park office and may be unavailable on weekends.

HIKING: Several marked trails. A trail map is available.

WINTER ACTIVITIES: Cross-country skiing.

For additional information:
Hunterdon County Department of Parks and Recreation
P.O. Box 2900
Flemington, NJ 08822–2900
Telephone: (908) 782-1158; Fax: (908) 806-4057

John A. Roebling Park

Sewell Avenue ♦ Hamilton Township, Mercer County ♦
257 acres

LOCATION: South of Route 206 (South Broad Street), and west of I–295.
Access from Sewell Avenue.

HOURS: Dawn to dusk.

ENTRANCE FEE: None.

HANDICAP ACCESS: None.

PICNICKING: A small picnic area is accessible from the Wescott Avenue
entrance.

BOATING: Allowed in 18-acre White City Lake. Car-top boat access; electric motors only.

FISHING: Permitted in the lake.

HIKING: Several walking paths.

For additional information:
Mercer County Park Commission
P.O. Box 8068
Trenton, NJ 08560
Telephone: (609) 989-6530

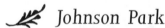

Johnson Park

River Road ♦ Piscataway, Middlesex County ♦ *473 acres*

LOCATION: Northwest of Highland Park, along the north shore of the
Raritan River. Access is from River Road.

HOURS: The grounds are open from dawn to dusk. East Jersey Olde
Town is open Tuesday through Friday, from 8:30 A.M. to 4:15 P.M.

ENTRANCE FEE: None.

HANDICAP ACCESS: East Jersey Olde Town is handicap accessible, as are
the restrooms.

East Jersey Olde Towne—A collection of original, replica, and recon-structed eighteenth- and nineteenth-century structures. For more information, call (732) 745-3030.

Animal Haven—An assortment of wild and farm animals in outside pens.

PICNICKING: Several shaded groves with tables and grills. Playground equipment, with restrooms nearby.

FISHING: Permitted in the ponds and in the Raritan River.

HIKING: The park is adjacent to the Delaware and Raritan Canal State Park, giving easy access and parking for the towpath.

WINTER ACTIVITIES: Cross-country skiing.

For additional information:
Middlesex County Department of Parks and Recreation
P.O. Box 661
New Brunswick, NJ 08903
Telephone: (732) 745-3900

Joseph Medwick Park

Post Boulevard ◆ Carteret, Middlesex County ◆ 82 acres

LOCATION: West of the New Jersey Turnpike, exit 12.

HOURS: Dawn to dusk.

ENTRANCE FEE: None.

HANDICAP ACCESS: The restrooms are handicap accessible.

PICNICKING: Two shaded groves and one open area located at the east-ern entrance to the park. Restrooms and a playground are located nearby.

FISHING: Permitted in the Rahway River.

WINTER ACTIVITIES: Cross-country skiing.

For additional information:
Middlesex County Department of Parks and Recreation
P.O. Box 661
New Brunswick, NJ 08903
Telephone: (732) 745-3900

Ken Lockwood Gorge
Wildlife Management Area

Raritan River Road ◆ *Califon Township,*
Hunterdon County ◆ *371 acres*

LOCATION: East of Voorhees State Park, north of High Bridge, and east of Route 513. From Route 639, turn north on Raritan River Road.

HOURS: Dawn to dusk.

ENTRANCE FEE: None.

HANDICAP ACCESS: None.

FISHING: Permitted in the South Branch of the Raritan River.

HIKING: Informal trails.

MOUNTAIN BIKING: Allowed on existing trails and secondary roads from March 1 to April 15, and from June 1 to September 15, as well as on all Sundays throughout the year.

HUNTING: For deer and small game.

WINTER ACTIVITIES: Cross-country skiing on all trails on Sunday.

Greg Johnson

Ken Lockwood Gorge Wildlife Management Area.

For additional information:
New Jersey Division of Fish and Wildlife
Trenton Office
501 E. State Street, P.O. Box 400
Trenton, NJ 08625–0400
Telephone: (609) 984-0547

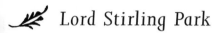 Lord Stirling Park

Basking Ridge, Somerset County ◆ *900 acres*

LOCATION: South of I–287, exit 26. Take I–287 to North Maple Avenue. Continue to South Maple Avenue, and turn east at Lord Stirling Road.

HOURS: The grounds are open from dawn to dusk. The Environmental Center is open daily, from 9:00 A.M. to 5:00 P.M.

ENTRANCE FEE: None.

HANDICAP ACCESS: A 1,200-foot trail for the handicapped is located at the Environmental Center. A riding program for the handicapped is also available at the stables.

SPECIAL FEATURES

Lord Stirling Stables—Conducts a full program of public riding and group instructional classes. Horses can be boarded and also rented at the stable. It is located at 256 South Maple Avenue, Basking Ridge. For more information, call (908) 766-5955.

Somerset County Environmental Center—Houses a large meeting room, classrooms, and natural history displays. An extensive library is open to the public. Two bird blinds are also open to the public. It is located at 190 Lord Stirling Road, Basking Ridge. For more information, call (908)766-2489.

BOATING: Nonmotorized craft are permitted in the park ponds. There is car-top access to the Passaic River for nonmotorized boats.

FISHING: Permitted in the ponds and in the Passaic River.

HIKING: Several marked trails, totaling more than eight and a half miles of trails, including almost three miles of boardwalk.

HORSEBACK RIDING: An extensive bridle trail system of more than four-teen miles.

BIRDWATCHING: There are two bird blinds.

WINTER ACTIVITIES: Cross-country skiing.

For additional information:
Somerset County Park Commission
P.O. Box 5327
North Branch, NJ 08876
Telephone: (908) 722-1200; Fax: (908) 722-6592

 # Mercer County Park

Old Trenton Road (Route 535), or Hughes Drive ◆
West Windsor Township, Mercer County ◆ 2,500+ acres

LOCATION: Take Route 1, east of I–295, to Quakerbridge Road (Route 533). Access is also from Route 130/33 to Windsor Road. The east entrance, on Edinburg Road (Route 526), gives access only to the east picnic area.

HOURS: Dawn to dusk.

ENTRANCE FEE: None.

HANDICAP ACCESS: The nature trail is handicap accessible.

Mercer County Park.

Greg Johnson

PICNICKING: The West Picnic Area is situated alongside Lake Mercer, within walking distance of the marina. There are more than 125 tables, some with grills, in wooded areas, open fields, and near the lake. Playground equipment and modern restrooms, as well as a public telephone, are available.

BOATING: The park has a marina on 300-acre Lake Mercer, with a boat ramp for trailer and car-top boats. It can be used during the hours when the park is open. The lake is open to the public from mid-April through October. Boats can also be rented. Gas motors are not permitted. For more information, call (609) 448-4004.

FISHING: Permitted in Lake Mercer.

HIKING: Several trails.

WINTER ACTIVITIES: Cross-country skiing can be enjoyed. In addition, an ice-skating rink is in operation from mid-November through mid-March, seven days a week. Skate rentals are available. For more information, call (609) 586-8090.

> **For additional information:**
> Mercer County Park Commission
> P.O. Box 8068
> Trenton, NJ 08560
> Telephone: (609) 989-6530

Merrill Park

Middlesex Turnpike ◆ Woodbridge Township,
Middlesex County ◆ 179 acres

LOCATION: Off Route 27, and east of the Garden State Parkway, exit 131.

HOURS: Dawn to dusk.

ENTRANCE FEE: None.

HANDICAP ACCESS: The restrooms are handicap accessible.

SPECIAL FEATURES
   Zoo—Small zoo with farm animals.

PICNICKING: Several groves with tables, some with grills. Restrooms are nearby.

HIKING: Informal trails.

WINTER ACTIVITIES: Cross-country skiing.

For additional information:
Middlesex County Department of Parks and Recreation
P.O. Box 661
New Brunswick, NJ 08903
Telephone: (732) 745-3900

 Musconetcong River Reservation

Musconetcong Gorge Section

Holland Township, Hunterdon County • 425 acres

LOCATION: West of Bloomsbury Boro, and adjacent to the Hunterdon County border with Warren County. From I–78, travel west to exit 7, and proceed to Route 173 west. Drive 1.3 miles to route 639. Turn left onto Route 639, and travel 4 miles. At the stop sign, bear left on Route 519, then turn left and cross the Musconetcong River, staying on Route 519. Take the next left onto Dennis Road, a gravel road, and go 0.2 miles to the parking area located on the left side of the road.

HOURS: Dawn to dusk.

ENTRANCE FEE: None.

HANDICAP ACCESS: None.

HIKING: Self-guided nature trail, in addition to several other marked trails.

FISHING: Permitted in the Musconetcong River.

HUNTING: Limited hunting for deer.

Note: Visitors to this park are requested to wear blaze orange during hunting season, or to confine their visits to Sunday.

Point Mountain Section

Lebanon Township, Hunterdon County • 756 acres

LOCATION: The park is located at the northernmost tip of the county. Parking is located on Penwell Road and Point Mountain Road.

HOURS: Dawn to dusk.

ENTRANCE FEE: None.

HANDICAP ACCESS: None.

FISHING: Permitted in the Musconetcong River for trout.

HIKING: Several marked trails, totaling more than four miles.

MOUNTAIN BIKING: Permitted on designated trails.

HORSEBACK RIDING: Permitted on designated trails.

WINTER ACTIVITIES: Cross-country skiing on designated trails.

For Additional information:
Hunterdon County Department of Parks and Recreation
P.O. Box 2900
Flemington, NJ 08822–2900
Telephone: (908) 782-1158; Fax: (908) 806-4057

 # North Branch Park

Milltown Road ◆ Bridgewater Township, Somerset County ◆
170 acres

LOCATION: From Route 202, west of Raritan, turn north onto Milltown
Road, and continue on to the park entrance.

HOURS: Dawn to dusk.

ENTRANCE FEE: None.

HANDICAP ACCESS: None.

PICNICKING: Two picnic groves, Brook Grove and River Grove. Both are
lightly wooded, with tables and grills, and with a large playground, restrooms, and a public telephone nearby.

FISHING: Permitted in the north branch of the Raritan River, which
borders the park.

For additional information:
Somerset County Park Commission
P.O. Box 5327
North Branch, NJ 08876
Telephone: (908) 722-1200; Fax: (908) 722-6592

Plainsboro Preserve

Plainsboro, Middlesex County ◆ *630 acres*

LOCATION: Follow Route 1 north or south to the Scudders Mills Road exit in Plainsboro Township. Exit onto Scudders Mills Road, and continue on to the traffic light at the intersection with Dey Road (County Route 614). Make a left onto Dey Road. Follow this to the first light, and make a left onto Scotts Corner Road. The Preserve entrance is one mile up, on the left.

HOURS: The grounds are open from dawn to dusk. The Nature Center is open Tuesday through Saturday, from 9:00 A.M. to 5:00 P.M., and on Sunday, from 12:00 P.M. to 5:00 P.M.

ENTRANCE FEE: None.

HANDICAP ACCESS: The Nature Center is handicap accessible.

SPECIAL FEATURES
Nature Center—Exhibits and displays of live animals, as well as information.

HIKING: Five miles of marked trails. A map is available.

> **For additional information:**
> *80 Scotts Corner Road*
> *P.O. Box 446*
> *Plainsboro, NJ 08536*
> *Telephone: (609) 897-9400*

 # Princeton Battlefield State Park

500 Mercer Street ◆ *Princeton, Mercer County* ◆
681 acres

LOCATION: Adjacent to Princeton Institute Woods. Access from Route 206, about 1.5 miles southwest of Princeton.

HOURS: The grounds are open from dawn to dusk. The Thomas Clarke house is open Wednesday through Saturday, from 10:00 A.M. to 12:00 P.M., and again from 1:00 P.M. to 4:00 P.M.; and on Sunday, from 1:00 P.M. to 4:00 P.M.

ENTRANCE FEE: None.

HANDICAP ACCESS: The first floor of the Thomas Clarke house and the restroom are handicap accessible.

Princeton Battlefield State Park.

DESCRIPTION: This park commemorates the historic Battle of Princeton, which took place on January 3, 1777, when General Washington led the American forces to victory. This battlefield is one of the few to remain virtually unchanged since the Revolution.

SPECIAL FEATURES

Thomas Clarke House—A pre-Revolutionary farmhouse that has been converted to a museum depicting eighteenth-century life.

HIKING: Numerous trails connect with the trails of the Princeton Institute Woods, and with the Delaware and Raritan Canal State Park.

WINTER ACTIVITIES: Cross-country skiing.

For additional information:
500 Mercer Street
Princeton, NJ 08540–4810
Telephone: (609) 921-0074

 Princeton Institute Woods

Olden Lane • Princeton, Mercer County • 550 *acres*

LOCATION: Take Route 1 to the traffic light at Alexander Road. Turn northwest, toward Princeton, and go almost 1 mile to West Drive, which leads to the preserve.

HOURS: The grounds are open from one hour before sunrise to one hour after sunset. The Institute reception desk is open for inquiries on weekdays, from 9:00 A.M. to 5:00 P.M.

ENTRANCE FEE: None.

HANDICAP ACCESS: None.

HIKING: Several trails wind through the woods. Of particular interest to children is a suspension bridge over Stony Brook. The bridge can be located by taking the trail that follows the brook. A brochure of the trails is available at the reception desk.

BIRDWATCHING: The Woods are a well-known birding spot.

WINTER ACTIVITIES: Cross-country skiing.

> **For additional information:**
> Institute for Advanced Study
> Olden Lane
> Princeton, NJ 08540
> Telephone: (609) 734-8000

 # Roosevelt Park

Oakwood Avenue ◆ *Edison, Middlesex County* ◆
217 acres

LOCATION: Located between Route 27 and Route 1, west of the Garden State Parkway.

HOURS: Dawn to dusk.

ENTRANCE FEE: None.

HANDICAP ACCESS: The playground and restrooms are handicap accessible.

PICNICKING: There are three main picnic groves. All are shaded, with tables, some with grills, and restrooms. Playgrounds are located at all of the groves. Grove 1, situated near the lake, has a small food concession.

FISHING: Permitted in the 10-acre lake.

HIKING: Informal trails.

WINTER ACTIVITIES: Cross-country skiing and ice skating.

For additional information:
Middlesex County Department of Parks and Recreation
P.O. Box 661
New Brunswick, NJ 08903
Telephone: (732) 745-3900

Rosedale Park

Blackwell Road • Hopewell, Mercer County • 472 acres

LOCATION: North of Route 546, and east of Route 31, about 1.5 miles east of Pennington.

HOURS: Open April through October, from 10:00 A.M. to dusk.

ENTRANCE FEE: None.

HANDICAP ACCESS: One of the toilets is handicap accessible.

PICNICKING: Situated alongside the lake, with tables and grills. A small playground is nearby. There are seasonal (nonflush) toilets.

BOATING: Allowed on the 38-acre lake. No gas motors.

FISHING: Permitted in the lake, which is stocked with trout.

For additional information:
Mercer County Park Commission
P.O. Box 8068
Trenton, NJ 08560
Telephone: (609) 989-6530

Round Valley Recreation Area

Lebanon Stanton Road (Route 629) • Lebanon,
Hunterdon County • 3,639 acres

LOCATION: South of Route 22, and east of Route 31.

HOURS: The grounds are open during the summer, from 8:00 A.M. to 8:00 P.M., and during the winter, from 8:00 A.M. to 4:30 P.M. The office is open during the summer, from 8:00 A.M. to 6:00 P.M., and during the winter, from 9:00 A.M. to 4:00 P.M.

ENTRANCE FEE: Fee charged from Memorial Day weekend through Labor Day.

HANDICAP ACCESS: Many of the facilities at the recreation area are handicap accessible.

CAMPING: Available all year. From November 1 through March 31, one-third of the sites are open, and from April 1 through October 31, all 116 wilderness campsites are open. The sites are spread over three and a half miles of the south and northeast shores of the reservoir. Access is by hiking (the trail is hilly) or boat only. The closest site is approximately three miles from the campers' parking lot. Each site is a twenty-by-twenty-foot clearing in the woods and contains a fire ring. Grills, tables, and benches are not provided. Drinking water and pit toilets are available at designated areas.

PICNICKING: There are three picnic areas, with tables and grills. Two are at wooded locations on each side of the swimming area, and the third is on a hill overlooking the park and reservoir.

BOATING: A boat launch is located near the campers' parking lot. Sailboats and canoes, and motorboats of up to 10 horsepower, are allowed. The maximum length of boats, including sailboats, is twenty-five feet.

SWIMMING: A sandy, lifeguard-supervised beach is open during the summer. Restrooms, changing rooms, lockers, first aid, and a food concession are available. Playgrounds are located at each end of the beach.

FISHING: Permitted in the 2,350-acre reservoir. Rainbow and brown trout are stocked yearly. Special regulations apply to fishing in the reservoir.

HIKING: There is a hiking trail that also serves the camping area. It is generally rugged and is not a loop (nine miles each way). The Pine Tree Trail, beginning at the south parking lot, is an easy one-mile loop trail.

MOUNTAIN BIKING: Permitted on the hiking trail.

HORSEBACK RIDING: Permitted on the hiking trail.

WINTER ACTIVITIES: An established ice-skating area is located at the east end of the beach complex. Other activities include sledding and cross-country skiing. Ice sailing and ice fishing are also possible when the reservoir is frozen.

HUNTING: Permitted in designated areas (2,350 acres), for waterfowl.

For additional information:
1220 Lebanon–Stanton Road
Lebanon, NJ 08833–3115
Telephone: (908) 236-6355

Scherman–Hoffman Sanctuaries

Hardscrabble Road ◆ Bernardsville ◆ 276 acres

LOCATION: North of Route 202, and east of Route 525, northeast of the town of Bernardsville.

HOURS: The grounds are open daily, from 9:00 A.M. to 5:00 P.M. The office is open Tuesday through Saturday, from 9:00 A.M. to 5:00 P.M.; and Sunday, from 12:00 P.M. to 5:00 P.M.

ENTRANCE FEE: None.

HANDICAP ACCESS: The Nature Center is handicap accessible.

SPECIAL FEATURES

Hoffman Nature Center—Exhibits, a book and gift shop, and a restroom.

HIKING: Several marked trails, ranging from 0.3 to 1.3 miles.

BIRDWATCHING: There is an observation deck.

For additional information:
11 Hardscrabble Road
P.O. Box 693
Bernardsville, NJ 07924
Telephone: (908) 766-5787; Fax: (908) 766-7775

Sourland Mountain Nature Preserve

Rileyville Road ◆ East Amwell Township,
Hunterdon County ◆ 273 acres

LOCATION: East of Route 514, on the Mercer County line.

HOURS: Dawn to dusk.

ENTRANCE FEE: None.

HANDICAP ACCESS: None.

HIKING: Two marked trails.

MOUNTAIN BIKING: Permitted on the trails.

HUNTING: For deer.

Note: Visitors to this park are requested to wear blaze orange during hunting season, or to confine their visits to Sunday.

For additional information:
Hunterdon County Department of Parks and Recreation
P.O. Box 2900
Flemington, NJ 08822–2900
Telephone: (908) 788-1158; Fax: (908) 806-4057

 # Sourland Mountain Preserve

Hillsborough and Montgomery Townships •
Somerset County • 2,835 acres

LOCATION: West of Route 206, and south of Amwell Road (Route 514). Access is from East Mountain Road.

HOURS: Dawn to dusk.

ENTRANCE FEE: None.

HANDICAP ACCESS: None.

HIKING: More than six miles of marked trails. A map is available.

MOUNTAIN BIKING: Permitted on trails.

HORSEBACK RIDING: Permitted on trails.

FISHING: Permitted in 0.75-acre pond.

WINTER ACTIVITIES: Cross-country skiing.

For additional information:
Somerset County Park Commission
P.O. Box 5327
North Branch, NJ 08876
Telephone: (908) 722-1200; Fax: (908) 722-6592

 # South Branch Reservation

Columbia Trail Section

High Bridge and Califon Boroughs, Clinton and Lebanon
Townships • Hunterdon County • 108 acres

LOCATION: The trailhead is in High Bridge, and the terminus of the trail is located on Valley Brook Road. Parking is available in the munic-

Pine Hill Road Bridge, South Branch Reservation.

ipal parking lot on Van Syckles Road, near the High Bridge borough hall.

HOURS: Dawn to dusk.

ENTRANCE FEE: None.

HANDICAP ACCESS: Although the trail is not specifically handicap accessible, it is wide and flat and easily negotiated.

HIKING: Seven-mile trail, with benches placed periodically for rest and enjoyment. Several roads bisect the park near the trail, making for easy trail access at various locations.

MOUNTAIN BIKING: Permitted on trail.

WINTER ACTIVITIES: Cross-country skiing.

Echo Hill Section

*Lilac Drive ◆ Clinton Township, Hunterdon County ◆
76 acres*

LOCATION: From the Clinton area, take Route 31 south about 6.2 miles, from I–78 to the traffic light for Stanton Station Road. Turn right onto Stanton Station Road. Travel 0.4 miles to Lilac Drive. At Lilac Drive, turn right and proceed another 0.4 miles. The entrance to the park will be on the right. Follow the sign to the main parking area.

HOURS: Dawn to dusk.

ENTRANCE FEE: None.

HANDICAP ACCESS: None.

PICNICKING: Tables, with grills, a playground, and a restroom.

FISHING: Permitted in 1-acre pond; catch and release.

HIKING: Marked trail.

MOUNTAIN BIKING: Permitted on the trail.

BIRDWATCHING: There is a seasonal bird blind overlooking the pond.

WINTER ACTIVITIES: Cross-country skiing.

Stanton Station Section

Stanton Station Road, Raritan Township ◆ *47 acres*

LOCATION: Take Route 31 north, about 5.6 miles, from the Flemington Circle. Make a right onto the jug handle for Stanton Station Road. The parking lot is one half mile down, on the left-hand side, just after the bridge.

HOURS: Dawn to dusk.

ENTRANCE FEE: None.

HANDICAP ACCESS: None.

FISHING: Permitted in the South Branch of the Raritan River.

HIKING: Marked trails.

MOUNTAIN BIKING: Permitted on trails.

HORSEBACK RIDING: Permitted on trails.

Sunnyside Picnic Area

Kiceniuk Road, Clinton Township ◆ *47 acres*

LOCATION: From the Flemington Circle, take Route 31 north about 5.6 miles, and make a right onto the jug handle for Stanton Station Road. Make the first right onto Lilac Drive. Travel approximately 1 mile, to Kiceniuk Road, and turn left. After crossing the railroad tracks, Kiceniuk bears to the right. Do not proceed straight and across the river; continue along Kiceniuk. The parking lot is on the left, just before the bridge.

HOURS: Dawn to dusk.

ENTRANCE FEE: None.

HANDICAP ACCESS: None.

PICNICKING: There are several sites along the river that have tables with grills; there is no restroom.

BOATING: Canoe access to the South Branch of the Raritan River.

FISHING: Permitted in the river, which is stocked with trout.

HIKING: Marked trail.

MOUNTAIN BIKING: Permitted on trail.

HORSEBACK RIDING: Permitted on trail.

WINTER ACTIVITIES: Cross-country skiing.

For additional information:
Hunterdon County Department of Parks and Recreation
P.O. Box 2900
Flemington, NJ 08822–2900
Telephone: (908) 788-1158; Fax: (908) 806-4057

Spring Lake Park

Plainfield Avenue ◆ *South Plainfield, Middlesex County* ◆
121 acres

LOCATION: North of Route 287, exit 4, and west of Route 531.

HOURS: Dawn to dusk.

ENTRANCE FEE: None.

HANDICAP ACCESS: The restrooms are handicap accessible.

FISHING: Permitted in the 5-acre lake.

WINTER ACTIVITIES: Ice skating.

For additional information:
Middlesex County Department of Parks and Recreation
P.O. Box 661
New Brunswick, NJ 08903
Telephone: (732) 745-3900

Spruce Run Recreation Area

Clinton, Hunterdon County ◆ *2,012 acres*

LOCATION: Located approximately 3.5 miles north of I–78, and just west of Route 31. From the intersections of I–78, exit 17, and Highway 31, follow 31 north. At the third traffic light, turn left. Continue on for 1.5 miles, and the entrance will be on the left.

HOURS: The grounds are open from dawn to dusk. The park office is open daily, Memorial Day weekend to Labor Day, from 8:00 A.M. to 8:00 P.M.; and the rest of the year, Monday through Friday, from 8:00 A.M. to 4:30 P.M.

ENTRANCE FEE: Fee charged from Memorial Day weekend to Labor Day.

HANDICAP ACCESS: The campground and picnic area are handicap accessible.

CAMPING: Seventy sites for tents and trailers. Each site has a table and fire ring. Facilities include modern restrooms with showers, outside running water, and a small playground. The camping season runs from April 1 through October 31.

Greg Johnson

Spruce Run Recreation Area.

PICNICKING: One picnic area is located before the beach area, and two more, with playgrounds, are between the beach and camping areas. Two additional picnic areas are located on the way to the boat launch. All have restrooms.

BOATING: The boathouse, located next to the camping area, is open from 7:00 A.M. to 6:00 P.M. on weekends, and from 8:00 A.M. to 6:00 P.M. on weekdays, only during the camping season. Boat rentals are available, and there is a public telephone. For more information, call (908) 638-8234. Boat launching facilities are available elsewhere in the park for trailer and car-top boats.

SWIMMING: A quarter-mile-long sand beach is provided with lifeguard supervision from Memorial Day weekend until Labor Day. Restrooms, changing rooms, first aid, and a food concession are provided. There is no playground.

FISHING: The 1,290-acre reservoir and its two feeder creeks offer excellent fishing. The reservoir is stocked with northern pike and with brown, rainbow, and brook trout.

HUNTING: Permitted in designated areas (1,300 acres), for waterfowl.

WINTER ACTIVITIES: Cross-country skiing and ice fishing.

For additional information:
One Van Syckels Road
Clinton, NJ 08809
Telephone: (908) 638-8572 or -8573

𝕶 Stony Brook—Millstone
Watershed Association Nature Preserve

31 Titus Mill Road ◆ Pennington, Mercer County ◆ 585 acres

LOCATION: From Route 31, north of Pennington, turn west onto Titus Mill Road.

HOURS: The grounds are open from dawn to dusk. The office is open Monday through Friday, from 9:00 A.M. to 5:00 P.M. The Education Nature Center is open Wednesday through Friday, from 10:00 A.M. to 5:00 P.M., and on Saturday, from 10:00 A.M. to 4:00 P.M.

ENTRANCE FEE: None.

HANDICAP ACCESS: The Education Nature Center is handicap accessible.

SPECIAL FEATURES

   Education Nature Center—Exhibits and displays of nature and art, and a discovery room for children. For more information, call (609) 737-7592.

HIKING: Six marked trails, totaling more than eight miles.

FISHING: Permitted in Stony Brook, and in the 4-acre pond.

WINTER ACTIVITIES: Cross-country skiing.

   For additional information:
   31 Titus Mill Road
   Pennington, NJ 08534
   Telephone (main office): (609) 737-3735; Fax: (609) 737-3075

 # Teetertown Ravine Nature Preserve

Hollowbrook Road and Pleasant Grove Road ◆
Lebanon Township, Hunterdon County ◆ 302 acres

Mountain Farm Section

LOCATION: Proceed north on Route 31, for 1.7 miles, to Route 513 north. Turn right, and follow Route 513 through High Bridge, toward Califon, for about 6.5 miles. Just past the A&P, turn left onto Sliker Road. After about 1.5 miles on Sliker Road, turn right onto Pleasant Grove Road, and travel another 0.6 miles. The driveway for Mountain Farm will be on the right-hand side.

HOURS: The grounds are open from dawn to dusk; the Visitor Center is open Saturday and Sunday, from 10:00 A.M. to 2:00 P.M.

ENTRANCE FEE: None.

HANDICAP ACCESS: The Visitor Center is handicap accessible.

SPECIAL FEATURES

   Visitor Center—Information and assistance to visitors. For more information, call (908) 832-7095.

CAMPING: Several tent sites, each with a table and fire ring. Pack in; pack out. There are portable toilets.

FISHING: Permitted in two ponds, catch and release, and in Hollow Brook, for native trout.

HIKING: Several marked trails, including a 0.8-mile geology trail.

MOUNTAIN BIKING: Permitted on trails.

HORSEBACK RIDING: Permitted on trails.

HUNTING: Limited deer hunting.

WINTER ACTIVITIES: Cross-country skiing.

Teetertown Ravine Section

LOCATION: Follow the directions above until having gone about 1.3 miles on Sliker Road. Then, turn right onto Teetertown Road. Follow the left fork of the road about 1 mile, to the stop sign at Hollow Brook Road. Turn left, and proceed 0.1 miles up the ravine. There are vehicle pull-offs near the trailheads.

HOURS: Dawn to dusk.

ENTRANCE FEE: None.

HANDICAP ACCESS: None.

HIKING: Several marked trails.

MOUNTAIN BIKING: Permitted on designated trails.

HORSEBACK RIDING: Permitted on designated trails.

HUNTING: Limited deer hunting.

WINTER ACTIVITIES: Cross-country skiing.

Note: Visitors to this park are requested to wear blaze orange during hunting season, or to confine their visits to Sunday.

For additional information:
Hunterdon County Department of Parks and Recreation
P.O. Box 2900
Flemington, NJ 08822–2900
Telephone: (908) 788-1158; Fax: (908) 806-4057

 # Thompson Park

Forsgate Drive ◆ *Jamesburg, Middlesex County* ◆
675 acres

LOCATION: Off Route 522, in Jamesburg.

HOURS: Dawn to dusk.

ENTRANCE FEE: None.

HANDICAP ACCESS: The restrooms are handicap accessible.

BOATING: Permitted in 30-acre Lake Manalapan. Electric motors only.

FISHING: Permitted in the lake.

HIKING: Unmarked trails.

PICNICKING: Several picnic groves are located in lightly wooded areas. All are provided with tables, some with grills. Restrooms and playgrounds are nearby.

WINTER ACTIVITIES: Ice skating and sledding (a designated sledding hill is maintained).

For additional information:
Middlesex County Department of Parks and Recreation
P.O. Box 661
New Brunswick, NJ 08903
Telephone: (732) 745-3900

 # Union Furnace Nature Preserve

Van Syckles Corner Road ◆ *Union Township,*
Hunterdon County ◆ *97 acres*

LOCATION: From the Flemington Circle, take Route 31 north 12.4 miles to Van Syckles Corner Road. Turn left, and go about 200 yards to Spruce Run's Fishing Access, which offers parking for the park. The entrance to the park is located on the opposite side of Van Syckles Corner Road.

HOURS: Dawn to dusk.

ENTRANCE FEE: None.

HANDICAP ACCESS: None.

FISHING: Permitted in Spruce Run Creek.

HIKING: A one and a half mile trail.

HUNTING: Limited hunting for deer.

Note: During hunting season, visitors to the park are asked to wear blaze orange, or to confine their visits to Sunday.

For additional information:
Hunterdon County Department of Parks and Recreation
P.O. Box 2900
Flemington, NJ 08822–2900
Telephone: (908) 788-1158; Fax: (908) 806-4057

 Voorhees State Park

Glen Gardner, Hunterdon County • 632 acres

LOCATION: Located in the wooded hills of northern Hunterdon County, 2 miles north of the town of High Bridge. From High Bridge, go north on County Road 513 (High Bridge–Long Valley Road), to the park entrance on the left side of the road. From I–78 (exit 17), take Route 31 north, to Route 513 north; or from Route 206 south, take Route 513 south.

HOURS: The grounds are open from dawn to dusk. The park office is open Memorial Day weekend to Labor Day, from 8:00 A.M. to 8:00 P.M., and during other times of the year, from 8:00 A.M. to 4:00 P.M. The Edwin E. Aldrin Astronomical Center is open from Memorial Day to October 31, every Saturday evening, from 8:30 P.M. to 10:30 P.M.; and every Sunday afternoon, from 2:00 P.M. to 5:00 P.M. From November 1 until Memorial Day, the Center is open every fourth Saturday, from 8:30 P.M. to 10:30 P.M. The Center is closed in December.

ENTRANCE FEE: None.

HANDICAP ACCESS: Camping, the picnic area, and restrooms are handicap accessible.

SPECIAL FEATURES

The Edwin E. Aldrin Astronomical Center—The center houses a lecture room with multimedia capabilities, a library, a photographic darkroom, and a sales counter where astronomically related items can be purchased. For more information, call (908) 638-8500.

CAMPING: Fifty tent and trailer sites are open all year. Each site has a table and fire ring. A modern restroom and showers are nearby. A trailer sanitary station is open from April 1 through October 31.

PICNICKING: Tables, with a playground and a restroom.

HIKING: Several marked trails, totaling six miles.

MOUNTAIN BIKING: Permitted on designated trails.

FISHING: Permitted in Willoughby Brook, for native trout.

HUNTING: Permitted in designated areas (300 acres), for deer, small game, and turkey.

WINTER ACTIVITIES: Cross-country skiing.

> **For additional information:**
> 251 Route 513
> Glen Gardner, NJ 08826
> Telephone: (908) 638-6969

Warren Park

> Florida Grove Road ◆ Woodbridge, Middlesex County ◆
> 126 acres

LOCATION: Located west of Route 35, and south of the New Jersey Turnpike, exit 11.

HOURS: Dawn to dusk.

ENTRANCE FEE: None.

HANDICAP ACCESS: The restrooms are handicap accessible.

HIKING: Informal walking trails.

PICNICKING: Tables are available, with grills; restrooms are nearby.

> **For additional information:**
> Middlesex County Department of Parks and Recreation
> P.O. Box 661
> New Brunswick, NJ 08903
> Telephone: (732) 745-3900

Washington Crossing State Park

> Route 546 ◆ Hopewell Township, Mercer County ◆
> 1,773 acres

LOCATION: Directly off the north side of Route 546, 0.5 miles west of Route 579. To get to the Washington Grove picnic area near the Delaware River, continue on Route 546 instead of entering the park. Pass through the intersection with Route 29, and keep to the right to enter the grove.

Washington Crossing State Park.

HOURS: The grounds are open from dawn to dusk. The Visitor Center is open daily, Memorial Day weekend through Labor Day, from 9:00 A.M. to 4:30 P.M., and during the rest of the year, Wednesday through Sunday, during the same hours. The Interpretive Center is open Wednesday through Saturday, from 9:00 A.M. to 4:30 P.M., and on Sunday, from 11:30 A.M. to 4:30 P.M.

ENTRANCE FEE: Fee charged from Memorial Day weekend to Labor Day. There is no charge for use of the Washington Grove picnic area.

HANDICAP ACCESS: The Visitor Center is handicap accessible.

DESCRIPTION: Did you know that almost three-quarters of the Revolutionary War was fought in New Jersey? Washington Crossing State Park commemorates Washington's crossing of the Delaware with his troops in 1776, to surprise and defeat the Hessians at Trenton and Princeton. These two battles are commonly considered the turning point of the Revolution. The park offers an excellent blend of history and nature, allowing visitors to spend time hiking, picnicking, and discovering the past.

SPECIAL FEATURES
Johnson Ferry House—This early eighteenth-century gambrel-roofed farmhouse and tavern near the Delaware River was owned by

Garret Johnson. Johnson operated a 490-acre Colonial plantation and a ferry service across the river in the 1700s. The house was likely used, briefly, by General Washington and other officers at the time of the Christmas-night crossing of the Delaware. The keeping room, bedchamber, and textile room are furnished with local period pieces, probably similar to the furniture used by the Johnson family from 1740 to 1770. The site also includes an eighteenth-century kitchen garden and an orchard of period fruit trees. Living history demonstrations are frequently held on weekends. For more information, call (609) 737-2515. Open Wednesday through Sunday, year-round.

Swan Historical Foundation Collection—The Swan collection represents a living military history laboratory of the American Revolution. More than 700 original objects interpret the era, circa 1745 through 1789. Open Wednesday through Sunday, year-round. For more information, call (609) 737-9303.

Interpretive Center—Exhibits and information about the park. For more information, call (609) 737-0609.

PICNICKING: There are four major picnic areas:

Knox Grove—Tables, some with grills, in a lightly wooded area. Modern restroom facilities and outside running water are provided. A playground is located nearby.

Green Grove—Tables, some with grills, in an open area with some trees. Modern restroom facilities and outside running water are provided. There is a playground.

Washington Grove—Large, lightly wooded area between the Delaware River and the canal. Tables, some with grills, outside running water, and a restroom are provided. A small playground is nearby.

Sullivan Grove—Located next to the Visitor Center in a lightly wooded area. Tables and a picnic shelter are available. A small playground is nearby, but no restrooms.

FISHING: Permitted in the Delaware River, and in the Delaware and Raritan Canal. Bass, shad, carp, and catfish, among others, may be found in the Delaware. The canal is stocked with trout in the spring.

HIKING: Thirteen miles of trails for hiking, walking, or jogging. There is also a one-quarter-mile, self-guided nature trail located near the Nature Center.

WINTER ACTIVITIES: Cross-country skiing and snowshoeing.

For additional information:
355 Washington Crossing-Pennington Road
Titusville, NJ 08560–1517
Telephone: (609) 737-0623

 # Washington Valley Park

Bridgewater Township, Somerset County   ◆   687 acres

LOCATION: North of Route 22, in the vicinity of Bound Brook. The park is bisected by Chimney Rock Road. Access is from Vosseller Avenue at Miller Lane, and also at Newman's Lane.

HOURS: Dawn to dusk.

ENTRANCE FEE: None.

HANDICAP ACCESS: None.

BOATING: Nonmotorized craft are allowed in the 21-acre reservoir. Walk-in access is about one-quarter of a mile from Newman's Lane parking lot.

FISHING: Permitted in the reservoir.

HIKING: Marked trails.

MOUNTAIN BIKING: Permitted on trails.

BIRDWATCHING: The park has a designated hawk-watch area.

For additional information:
Somerset County Park Commission
P.O. Box 5327
North Branch, NJ 08876
Telephone: (908) 722-1200; Fax: (908) 722-6592

Region Four

Monmouth & Ocean Counties

Monmouth County Park System

Seven Presidents' Oceanfront Park.

MONMOUTH

OCEAN

36

GSP

18

36

19

17

14

37

29

RED BANK

36

32

FREEHOLD

10

18

27

34

33

9

33

35

537

538

39

24

2

3

195

25

20

7

28

5

30

22

POINT
PLEASANT

LAKEWOOD

9

571

26

8

LAKEHURST

42

40

TOMS RIVER

530

37

539

11

13

6
12

16

9

21

41

31

554

4

BARNEGAT

1

34

72

23

35

TUCKERTON

15

#	Parks
•	Selected Towns
	Selected Roads
	County Borders

0   5
miles

-N-

Mike Siegel, Rutgers Cartography

154

1   A. Paul King Park
2   Allaire State Park
3   Assunpink Wildlife Management Area
4   Barnegat Lighthouse State Park
5   Beaver Dam Creek County Park
6   Berkeley Island County Park
7   Butterfly Bogs Wildlife Management Area
8   Cattus Island County Park
9   Colliers Mills Wildlife Management Area
10 Dorbrook Recreation Area
11 Double Trouble State Park
12 Eno's Pond County Park
13 Forked River Mountain Wildlife Management Area
14 Gateway National Recreation Area—Sandy Hook Unit
15 Great Bay Boulevard Wildlife Management Area
16 Greenwood Forest Wildlife Management Area
17 Hartshorne Woods Park
18 Holmdel Park
19 Huber Woods Park
20 Imlaystown Lake Wildlife Management Area
21 Island Beach State Park
22 Lake Shenandoah County Park
23 Manahawkin Wildlife Management Area
24 Manasquan Reservoir
25 Manasquan River Wildlife Management Area
26 Manchester Wildlife Management Area
27 Monmouth Battlefield State Park
28 Ocean County Park
29 Poricy Park
30 Prospertown Lake Wildlife Management Area
31 Sedge Islands Wildlife Management Area
32 Seven Presidents Oceanfront Park
33 Shark River Park
34 Stafford Forge Wildlife Management Area
35 Stanley "Tip" Seaman County Park
36 Tatum Park
37 Thompson Park
38 Turkey Swamp Park
39 Turkey Swamp Wildlife Management Area
40 Upper Barnegat Bay Wildlife Management Area
41 Wells Mills County Park
42 Whiting Wildlife Management Area

A. Paul King Park

Route 72 ◆ Stafford Township, Ocean County ◆ 48 acres

LOCATION: Off Route 72, just west of Route 9.

HOURS: Dawn to dusk.

ENTRANCE FEE: None.

HANDICAP ACCESS: The beach and the picnic area are handicap accessible.

DESCRIPTION: Though limited in size, this park offers a break from the shore for those traveling to the mainland from Long Beach Island.

PICNICKING: A shady picnic area with grills. A playground and restrooms are nearby.

FISHING: Permitted in Lake Manahawkin.

SWIMMING: A lifeguard-supervised, sand beach is open, mid-June through Labor Day, from 10:00 A.M. to 6:00 P.M.

> **For additional information:**
> *Ocean County Parks and Recreation Department*
> *1198 Brandon Road*
> *Toms River, NJ 08753*
> *Telephone: (732) 506-9090*

Allaire State Park

Allaire Road (Route 524) ◆ Monmouth County ◆
3,086 acres

LOCATION: Take the Garden State Parkway, exit 98, to I–195. Go west on I–195 for about 3 miles, to exit 31B (Route 547). Turn north on Route 547, and go a couple of hundred yards to Allaire Road.

HOURS: The grounds are open from dawn to dusk. The park office is open, Memorial Day weekend to Labor Day, from 8:00 A.M. to 8:00 P.M.; in the spring and fall, from 8:00 A.M. to 6:00 P.M.; and in the winter, from 8:00 A.M. to 4:30 P.M. The Interpretive Center is open daily in the summer, from 9:00 A.M. to 4:30 P.M.; and in the winter, Wednesday through Sunday, from 9:00 A.M. to 4:00 P.M. Pine Creek Railroad is open, mid-June through Labor Day, spring and fall, and on weekends, from 12:00 P.M. to 4:00 P.M.

Allaire State Park.

Greg Johnson

ENTRANCE FEE: Fee charged from Memorial Day weekend to Labor Day.

HANDICAP ACCESS: Both yurts are handicap accessible.

SPECIAL FEATURES

Allaire Village—Originally settled in 1750, and known as Monmouth Furnace, the area became the site of a bog-ore furnace and forge, where iron ore was smelted and made into various products and utensils. During its heyday, in the first half of the 1800s, as many as four hundred people were living in the village, which contained more than sixty structures. Many of these structures are still standing and present an exciting glimpse into the past. For more information, write, or call Allaire Village for a calendar of events at (732) 938-2253.

Pine Creek Railroad—A working example of the type of travel used to open up the frontier. It is the only narrow-gauge steam train in New Jersey. For more information, call (732) 938-5524.

Interpretive Center—Displays and exhibits of plants and animals from the area. For more information, call (732) 938-2003.

YURTS: There are two yurts: circular tents built on a wood frame, featuring wood floors, a deck, and a Plexiglas skylight. Each yurt has a lockable wood door, window screens and flaps, and two double-deck bunks, which sleep up to four people. Accessible to people with disabilities.

CAMPING: Fifty-five wooded sites for family camping (trailers and tents), each with a picnic table and fire ring. The area is heavily forested. Facilities include modern restrooms, hot showers, a dumping station, and clothes washers and dryers. A trailer sanitary station is available from April 1 through October 31; campsites are open year-round.

PICNICKING: Located near Allaire Village, with restrooms and a playground nearby.

BOATING: Canoeing is allowed in the Manasquan River. Canoe rentals are available nearby.

FISHING: Permitted in the Mingemanhone and Manasquan Rivers, both of which are stocked annually with trout. In Allaire Village, the Lower Mill Pond is open to fishing for children and is stocked with various species of pan fish.

HIKING: Miles of marked trails and roads appropriate for hiking.

MOUNTAIN BIKING: Permitted on designated trails.

HORSEBACK RIDING: Permitted on designated trails.

HUNTING: Permitted in designated areas (870 acres), for deer.

WINTER ACTIVITIES: Cross-country skiing.

> **For additional information:**
> P.O. Box 220
> Farmingdale, NJ 07727
> Telephone: (732) 938-2371

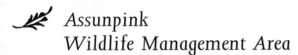

Assunpink
Wildlife Management Area

Imlaystown Road • 5,746 acres

LOCATION: Take I–195 to exit 11 (Imlaystown Road), and head north. The paved road will turn into a dirt road and will eventually lead to Assunpink Lake.

HOURS: Dawn to dusk.

ENTRANCE FEE: None.

HANDICAP ACCESS: None.

DESCRIPTION: In addition to excellent fishing, Assunpink Wildlife Management Area offers some of the best birdwatching in central New Jersey.

BOATING: Launching facilities for both car-top and trailer boats at 225-acre Assunpink Lake, 38-acre Rising Sun Lake, and 52-acre Stone Tavern Lake. No gas motors are permitted.

FISHING: Excellent fishing for a number of fish, including largemouth bass, channel catfish, chain pickerel, and bluegill.

HIKING: Informal trails.

MOUNTAIN BIKING: Allowed on existing trails and secondary roads from March 1 to April 15, and from June 1 to September 15, as well as on all Sundays throughout the year.

HUNTING: For deer, small game, turkey, and waterfowl.

WINTER ACTIVITIES: Cross-country skiing on all trails on Sunday.

Assunpink Wildlife Management Area.

For additional information:
New Jersey Division of Fish and Wildlife
Trenton Office
501 E. State Street, P.O. Box 400
Trenton, NJ 08625–0400
Telephone: (609) 984-0547

 ## Barnegat Lighthouse State Park

Broadway, Barnegat Light • *32 acres*

LOCATION: At the northern tip of Long Beach Island. Take Route 72 to Long Beach Island, and then go north toward Barnegat Light.

HOURS: The grounds open at 8:00 A.M., and closing times vary according to the season. The lighthouse is open periodically in the evening during the summer. Call the park office for times.

ENTRANCE FEE: None.

HANDICAP ACCESS: A 1,033-foot concrete walkway with handrails atop the south jetty provides fishing access for people with disabilities. The picnic areas are also handicap accessible.

PICNICKING: An unshaded picnic area is located near the lighthouse. Picnic tables are also available under two sun shelters. No grills are permitted.

FISHING: Permitted in the ocean. Saltwater anglers have access to the bulkhead along the picnic area, where they can catch striped bass, bluefish, weakfish, summer flounder, winter flounder, and black bass.

For additional information:
P.O. Box 167
Barnegat Light, NJ 08006
Telephone: (609) 494-2016

 ## Beaver Dam Creek County Park

Bridge Avenue • *Point Pleasant, Ocean County* • *40 acres*

LOCATION: North of Route 88, and west of Bridge Avenue.

HOURS: Dawn to dusk.

ENTRANCE FEE: None.

HANDICAP ACCESS: The picnic area is handicap accessible.

PICNICKING: Tables with grills, with a playground and a restroom.

HIKING: Trail with boardwalk through tidal wetlands.

For additional information:

Ocean County Parks and Recreation Department
1198 Brandon Road
Toms River, NJ 08753
Telephone: (732) 506-9090

 # Berkeley Island County Park

Brennan Concourse ◆ Cedar Beach, Ocean County ◆
25 *acres*

LOCATION: East of Route 9, and south of Route 618 (Butler Boulevard).

Take the Garden State Parkway north/south to exit 74. Go east on Lacey Road to Route 9, and then head north on Route 9. Make a right, heading east, onto Harbor Inn Road. Turn left at Neary Avenue, and then right on Brennan Concourse, and proceed to the park entrance.

HOURS: Dawn to dusk.

ENTRANCE FEE: None.

Ocean County Parks and Recreation, Catherine L. King

Berkeley Island County Park.

HANDICAP ACCESS: The fishing/crabbing pier and the picnic area are handicap accessible.

PICNICKING: Available, with grills, with a playground and a restroom.

FISHING: Permitted on one-hundred-foot pier.

CRABBING: Permitted on one-hundred-foot pier.

SWIMMING: Available, mid-June to Labor Day, from 10:00 A.M. to 6:00 P.M. A restroom is near the beach.

For additional information:
Ocean County Parks and Recreation Department
1198 Brandon Road
Toms River, NJ 08753
Telephone: (732) 506-9090

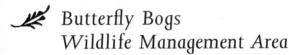

Butterfly Bogs
Wildlife Management Area

Butterfly Road • Jackson Township, Monmouth County •
103 acres

LOCATION: From Route 527/528, south of Holmansville, turn east onto Butterfly Road for access roads into the tract.

HOURS: Dawn to dusk.

ENTRANCE FEE: None.

HANDICAP ACCESS: None.

FISHING: Permitted in three lakes, where there is good pickerel and catfish fishing.

MOUNTAIN BIKING: Allowed on existing trails and secondary roads from March 1 to April 15, and from June 1 to September 15, as well as on all Sundays throughout the year.

HUNTING: For deer and small game.

WINTER ACTIVITIES: Cross-country skiing on all trails on Sunday.

For additional information:
New Jersey Division of Fish and Wildlife
Trenton Office
501 E. State Street, P.O. Box 400
Trenton, NJ 08625–0400
Telephone: (609) 984-0547

Cattus Island County Park

1170 Cattus Island Boulevard • Toms River,
Ocean County • 400 acres

LOCATION: East of Spur 549 (Fischer Boulevard), and north of Route 571 (Bay Avenue).

HOURS: The grounds are open from dawn to dusk. The Nature Center is open daily, from 8:30 A.M. to 4:30 P.M.

ENTRANCE FEE: None.

HANDICAP ACCESS: The Nature Center is handicap accessible. A boardwalk trail is also accessible.

SPECIAL FEATURES

Cooper Environmental Center—Includes an eighty-seat meeting room, exhibit area, library, darkroom, and restrooms. There are displays of live turtles, snakes, and fish in the exhibit area. For more information, call (732) 270-6960.

PICNICKING: Tables with grills and a playground. A restroom is nearby.

HIKING: Six miles of marked trails, and a one-mile fire road.

WINTER ACTIVITIES: Cross-country skiing.

> **For additional information:**
> *Ocean County Parks and Recreation Department*
> *1198 Brandon Road*
> *Toms River, NJ 08753*
> *Telephone: (732) 506-9090*

Colliers Mills Wildlife Management Area

Hawkins Road • Colliers Mills, Ocean County •
12,626 acres

LOCATION: East of Route 539, and south of Route 528. The office is located on Hawkins Road, east of Route 539.

HOURS: Dawn to dusk.

ENTRANCE FEE: None.

HANDICAP ACCESS: None.

BOATING: Car-top boat launch at 17-acre Colliers Mills Pond, and at 100-acre Turn Mill Pond.

FISHING: Permitted in three lakes.

HIKING: Informal trails and sand roads.

MOUNTAIN BIKING: Allowed on existing trails and secondary roads from March 1 to April 15, and from June 1 to September 15, as well as on all Sundays throughout the year.

HORSEBACK RIDING: Allowed on trails and sand roads, with a permit.

HUNTING: For deer, small game, turkey, and waterfowl.

WINTER ACTIVITIES: Cross-country skiing on all trails on Sunday.

> **For additional information:**
> New Jersey Division of Fish and Wildlife
> Trenton Office
> 501 E. State Street, P.O. Box 400
> Trenton, NJ 08625—0400
> Telephone: (609) 984-0547

 # Dorbrook Recreation Area

Colts Neck, Monmouth County • 534 acres

LOCATION: On the north side of Route 537, in Colts Neck.

HOURS: The grounds are open from dawn to dusk; the Visitor Center is open, Monday through Friday, from 8:00 A.M. to 4:30 P.M.

ENTRANCE FEE: None.

HANDICAP ACCESS: The Visitor Center, picnic area, and restrooms are handicap accessible.

SPECIAL FEATURES

Visitor Center—Information available on organized activities and on park facilities. For more information, call (732) 542-1642.

PICNICKING: Tables, no grills, with restrooms nearby.

HIKING: Informal trails, and 1.8 miles of paved trail for walking or biking.

WINTER ACTIVITIES: Cross-country skiing.

> **For additional information:**
> Monmouth County Park System
> 805 Newman Springs Road
> Lincroft, NJ 07738
> Telephone: (908) 842-4000

Double Trouble State Park

Double Trouble Road ◆ *Lacey and Berkeley Townships* ◆
Ocean County ◆ *7,336 acres*

LOCATION: From the Garden State Parkway, take exit 80. Turn south onto Double Trouble Road, and continue approximately 4 miles to the park entrance.

HOURS: The grounds are open from dawn to dusk; the park office is open daily, from 7:30 A.M. to 3:30 P.M.

ENTRANCE FEE: None.

HANDICAP ACCESS: None.

DESCRIPTION: Named after the eighteenth-century village of Double Trouble, which centered around timbering and cranberry cultivation. Consists of flat, wooded pinelands habitat and freshwater wetlands. Generally undeveloped.

SPECIAL FEATURES

Double Trouble Village—Located near the entrance to the park, the village (fourteen structures) provides a compact view of a self-contained cranberry production community.

Double Trouble State Park.

BOATING: Canoeing is allowed on a ten-mile stretch of Cedar Creek.

FISHING: Permitted in Cedar Creek, for pickerel.

HIKING: Twelve miles of tails and sand roads, including a one-mile, self-guided nature trail that includes both natural and historical items of interest. Brochure available.

MOUNTAIN BIKING: Permitted on sand roads.

HORSEBACK RIDING: Permitted on sand roads.

HUNTING: Permitted in designated areas (5,665 acres), for deer, small game, turkey, and waterfowl.

WINTER ACTIVITIES: Cross-country skiing.

For additional information:
PO Box 175,
Bayville, NJ 08721
Telephone: (732) 341-6662

 # Eno's Pond County Park

East Lacey Road • Lacey Township, Ocean County •
28 acres

LOCATION: Take the Garden State Parkway to exit 74 (Lacey Township). Travel east on Lacey Road for about 2.5 miles. Continue on across Route 9, onto East Lacey Road for approximately a mile. The park entrance is about 0.25 miles beyond "Captain's Inn" on the left.

HOURS: Dawn to dusk.

ENTRANCE FEE: None.

HANDICAP ACCESS: The pond observation area is handicap accessible.

PICNICKING: Tables with grills, with a playground and a restroom.

HIKING: Nature trails.

For additional information:
Ocean County Parks and Recreation Department
1198 Brandon Road
Toms River, NJ 08753
Telephone: (732) 506-9090

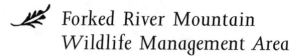

Forked River Mountain Wildlife Management Area

Ocean County ♦ *3,605 acres*

HOURS: Dawn to dusk.

ENTRANCE FEE: None.

HANDICAP ACCESS: None.

LOCATION: Located west of the Garden State Parkway, exit 74.

HIKING: Informal trails and sand roads.

MOUNTAIN BIKING: Allowed on existing trails and secondary roads from March 1 to April 15, and from June 1 to September 15, as well as on all Sundays throughout the year.

HUNTING: For deer, small game, and turkey.

WINTER ACTIVITIES: Cross-country skiing on all trails on Sunday.

> **For additional information:**
> *New Jersey Division of Fish and Wildlife*
> *Trenton Office*
> *501 E. State Street, P.O. Box 400*
> *Trenton, NJ 08625–0400*
> *Telephone: (609) 984-0547*

Gateway National Recreation Area— Sandy Hook Unit

Monmouth County ♦ *1,660 acres*

LOCATION: Located north of Route 36, near the town of Highlands.

HOURS: The grounds are open from dawn to dusk. The Visitor Center is open daily, from 10:00 A.M. to 5:00 P.M. The Fort Hancock Museum is open year-round, on weekends, from 1:00 P.M. to 5:00 P.M.

ENTRANCE FEE: Fee charged from Memorial Day weekend through Labor Day.

HANDICAP ACCESS: The restrooms are handicap accessible; beach wheelchairs are available (call ahead); and some areas have boardwalks to the beach.

DESCRIPTION: The holly forest is unsurpassed on the eastern seaboard (guided tours only). The park also has the oldest operating lighthouse in the country.

SPECIAL FEATURES

Fort Hancock—The last of several forts erected on Sandy Hook at the turn of the century, to protect the shipping channels into New York Harbor. Closed in 1973, it is now a museum.

Sandy Hook Bird Observatory—Promotes birding, natural history, environmental education, and conservation. For more information, call (732) 872-2500; or visit www.njaudubon.org/Centers/SHBO.

Spermaceti Cove Visitor Center—Housed in a former U.S. Lifesaving station, built in 1894, the center contains exhibit areas with information on area history and on flora and fauna. There is also a bookstore, restrooms, and drinking water. For more information, call (732) 872-5970.

PICNICKING: Tables and some grills are located at Guardian Park, near the bay side, at the beginning of Fort Hancock. This is the only area available for grilling; visitors are encouraged to bring their own grills, as they are limited.

FISHING: Permitted at nonguarded beaches. A nighttime fishing pass (nominal charge), valid from sunset to sunrise, may be obtained at the ranger station. No tents or camping permitted.

SWIMMING: Ocean swimming. Developed areas have restrooms, outside showers, and a concession.

HIKING: There are several trails at the park, including the one-mile Old Dune Trail (brochure available) that begins near the Visitor Center.

> **For additional information:**
> P.O. Box 530
> Fort Hancock, NJ 07732
> Telephone: (732) 872-5970

Great Bay Boulevard Wildlife Management Area

Great Bay Boulevard ◆ Tuckerton ◆ *5,282 acres*

LOCATION: From Route 9, near Tuckerton, turn south onto Great Bay Boulevard, and into the tract.

HOURS: Dawn to dusk.

ENTRANCE FEE: None.

HANDICAP ACCESS: None.

BOATING: Launching ramps are available, and several boat liveries are located along Great Bay Boulevard.

FISHING: Excellent saltwater fishing for species that include striped bass, weakfish, fluke, flounder, white perch, sea bass, shark, and bluefish.

CRABBING: Permitted in all waters.

CLAMMING: Permitted in all waters.

HUNTING: For waterfowl.

> **For additional information:**
> New Jersey Division of Fish and Wildlife
> Trenton Office
> 501 E. State Street, P.O. Box 400
> Trenton, NJ 08625−0400
> Telephone: (609) 984-0547

 # Greenwood Forest
Wildlife Management Area

Ocean County ◆ *28,727 acres*

LOCATION: North of Route 72, and south of Route 70. The tract is bisected by Route 539.

HOURS: Dawn to dusk.

ENTRANCE FEE: None.

HANDICAP ACCESS: None.

FISHING: Permitted in three small lakes.

HIKING: There is a boardwalk trail off of Route 539, and there are informal trails and sand roads.

MOUNTAIN BIKING: Allowed on existing trails and secondary roads from March 1 to April 15, and from June 1 to September 15, as well as on all Sundays throughout the year.

HORSEBACK RIDING: Allowed on all trails, with a permit.

HUNTING: For deer, small game, turkey, and waterfowl.

WINTER ACTIVITIES: Cross-country skiing on all trails on Sunday.

For additional information:
New Jersey Division of Fish and Wildlife
Trenton Office
501 E. State Street, P.O. Box 400
Trenton, NJ 08625–0400
Telephone: (609) 984-0547

 # Hartshorne Woods Park

Middletown, Monmouth County • *736 acres*

LOCATION: Take State Highway 35 to Navesink River Road, and continue 4.7 miles. Turn right onto Locust Road. Cross Clay Pit Creek Bridge to five-way intersection. Bear right onto Navesink Avenue, and continue on to the park.

HOURS: Dawn to dusk.

ENTRANCE FEE: None.

HANDICAP ACCESS: None.

FISHING: Permitted in the Navesink River.

HIKING: Fifteen miles of marked trails, including a three-mile paved trail.

MOUNTAIN BIKING: Permitted on designated trails.

HORSEBACK RIDING: Permitted on designated trails.

WINTER ACTIVITIES: Cross-country skiing.

For additional information:
Monmouth County Park System
805 Newman Springs Road
Lincroft, NJ 07738
Telephone: (732) 842-4000

 # Holmdel Park

Longstreet Road • Holmdel, Monmouth County •
343 acres

LOCATION: Located southwest of the Garden State Parkway, exit 116.

HOURS: The grounds are open from dawn to dusk; the office is open, Monday through Friday, from 8:00 A.M. to 4:30 P.M. Longstreet

Holmdel Park.

Farm is open daily, from Memorial Day weekend to Labor Day, from 9:00 A.M. to 5:00 P.M., and at all other times, daily, from 10:00 A.M. to 4:00 P.M.

ENTRANCE FEE: None.

HANDICAP ACCESS: Longstreet Farm is handicap accessible.

SPECIAL FEATURES
Longstreet Farm—A 9-acre living history farm, restored and maintained to represent the period of the 1890s. For more information, call (732) 946-3758.

PICNICKING: Picnic area with tables, grills, a playground, and a restroom.

FISHING: The lake is stocked with trout and channel catfish.

HIKING: Several marked trails of varying lengths.

WINTER ACTIVITIES: Cross-country skiing, ice skating, and sledding.

For additional information:
Monmouth County Park System
805 Newman Springs Road
Lincroft, NJ 07738
Telephone: (732) 842-4000

Monmouth County Park System

Longstreet Farm, Holmdel Park.

Monmouth County Park System

Fishing pond, Holmdel Park.

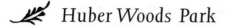 # Huber Woods Park

Middletown Township, Monmouth County • *258 acres*

LOCATION: South of Route 36, north of the Navesink River, and west of Hartshorne.

HOURS: The grounds are open from dawn to dusk. The Environmental Center is open weekdays, from 10:00 A.M. to 4:00 P.M., and on weekends, from 10:00 A.M. to 5:00 P.M. During the winter months, the Center closes at 4:00 P.M. on weekends.

ENTRANCE FEE: None.

HANDICAP ACCESS: The Environmental Center is handicap accessible.

SPECIAL FEATURES

Huber Woods Environmental Center—Hands-on nature and history displays. The restrooms at the center have outside access, and are closed at dusk. For more information, call (732) 872-2670.

PICNICKING: Tables scattered throughout the park, no grills.

HIKING: Extensive system of marked trails, including seven miles of multi-use trail.

MOUNTAIN BIKING: On the multi-use trail.

HORSEBACK RIDING: On the multi-use trail.

BIRDWATCHING: The Environmental Center has a bird-viewing area.

For additional information:
Monmouth County Park System
805 Newman Springs Road
Lincroft, NJ 07738
Telephone: (732) 842-4000

 # Imlaystown Lake
Wildlife Management Area

Monmouth County • *30 acres*

LOCATION: Located south of Route 526, in Imlaystown.

HOURS: Dawn to dusk.

ENTRANCE FEE: None.

HANDICAP ACCESS: None.

FISHING: Permitted in the lake.

For additional information:
New Jersey Division of Fish and Wildlife
Trenton Office
501 E. State Street, P.O. Box 400
Trenton, NJ 08625–0400
Telephone: (609) 984-0547

 Island Beach State Park

*Central Avenue • Seaside Park, Ocean County •
3,002 acres*

LOCATION: Take Route 37 east, to Central Avenue, heading south.

HOURS: The grounds are open from dawn to dusk. The park office is open from 8:00 A.M. to 6:00 P.M. during the summer, and from 8:00 A.M. to 4:30 P.M. during the rest of the year. The Nature Center is open from 9:00 A.M. to 4:00 P.M. during the summer. Call for winter hours.

ENTRANCE FEE: A fee is charged at all times, adjusted seasonally. If you plan on making regular visits to the park, a state park pass is advisable (see Introduction).

Greg Johnson

Island Beach State Park.

HANDICAP ACCESS: Much of the park is handicap accessible, including the beach (for swimming and fishing) and the restrooms. Access to the bathing beach is provided through use of portable walkways. Beach wheelchairs are also available.

DESCRIPTION: Island Beach State Park is one of the last undeveloped and relatively undisturbed barrier islands on the East Coast. It is divided into a northern and southern zone natural area, and a central recreational zone. The land, formerly owned by Henry Phipps, a Pittsburgh steel magnate, was purchased by the state in 1953. The park was opened in 1959.

SPECIAL FEATURES
Nature Center—Butterfly garden, live fish, displays, and exhibits of flora and fauna of the area. For more information, call (732) 793-1698.

PICNICKING: There are no established picnic areas; however, visitors may picnic on the ocean beach. Grills may be used on the beach south of the bathing area. Fires must be fifty feet east of the sand dune line on the beach.

BOATING: Limited car-top boat access to the bay.

FISHING: Excellent surf fishing. Bait can be obtained at local tackle dealers before entering the park. Special permits, both three-day and annual, are available for operating four-wheel-drive vehicles on the ocean beach for sport-fishing purposes only.

SWIMMING: Approximately one mile of beach is serviced by two bathing areas, each with its own facilities, and each accommodating about nine hundred cars. From mid-June until Labor Day, the beach is supervised by lifeguards. Parking is convenient to the beach, and there are changing areas, restrooms, a first-aid station, and a food and beach-supply concession.

HIKING: Seven marked trails, ranging from 0.1 to 0.5 miles in length.

HORSEBACK RIDING: Six miles of ocean beach in the central and southern areas are open to horseback riding from October 1 through April 30. No horse rental facilities are in or near the park, and there is a daily limit on the number of riders. A five-day advance reservation is required.

BIRDWATCHING: A bird blind is located on the bay side of the park.

SURFING: A portion of beach at the extreme southern area of the bathing beach, Unit 2, has been set aside for surfing.

SCUBA DIVING AND UNDERWATER FISHING: Permitted along two-and-a-half miles of ocean beach just north of the Barnegat Inlet. Scuba divers must register at the park office prior to their first dive each year and show proof of current diving certification.

HUNTING: Permitted in designated areas (300 acres), for waterfowl.

Note: Especially on weekends and holidays, it is worthwhile to arrive at the park as early as possible (before 9:30 A.M.). When the parking lots are full, the park is closed. Access is usually permitted again when people begin to leave the park, usually some time between 1:30 P.M. and 2:30 P.M.

For additional information:
P.O. Box 37
Seaside Park, NJ 08752
Telephone: (732) 793-0506

 # Lake Shenandoah County Park

Ocean Avenue (Route 88) ◆ Lakewood, Ocean County ◆ 143 acres

LOCATION: Between Route 88 and Route 528, west of the Garden State Parkway, exit 90. From the Garden State Parkway southbound, take exit 91 (Route 549/Lanes Mill Road) south to Route 88. Then travel west on Route 88, for about 2 miles, to the park entrance on the right. From the Garden State Parkway northbound, take exit 90 (Route 549/Chambers Bridge Road) to the jug handle for the U-turn. Travel north, about 0.5 miles, to Route 88. Travel west on Route 88, about 2 miles, to the park entrance on the left.

HOURS: The grounds are open from dawn to dusk; the bait and tackle shop is open daily, March through October, from 7:00 A.M. to 6:00 P.M.

ENTRANCE FEE: None.

HANDICAP ACCESS: The fishing piers and the picnic area are handicap accessible.

PICNICKING: There is a picnic area with restrooms.

BOATING: Small boat launch and boat rentals (paddle boats, rowboats, and canoes) are provided on the one-hundred-acre lake. Electric motors only.

FISHING: There are three fishing piers. The lake is stocked annually with trout. A bait and tackle shop is located at the park, and a modern restroom is located next to the shop. For more information, call (732) 363-9678.

> **For additional information:**
> Ocean County Parks and Recreation Department
> 1198 Brandon Road
> Toms River, NJ 08753
> Telephone: 732 506-9090

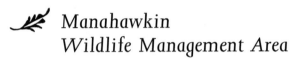

Manahawkin
Wildlife Management Area

Stafford Avenue, Stafford Township • *1,047 acres*

LOCATION: Located east of Route 9, and north of Route 72.

HOURS: Dawn to dusk.

ENTRANCE FEE: None.

HANDICAP ACCESS: None.

FISHING: Permitted in various locations throughout the tract, as well as in Cedar Creek, which is accessible from Stafford Avenue.

CRABBING: Permitted in Cedar Creek.

MOUNTAIN BIKING: Allowed on existing trails and secondary roads from March 1 to April 15, and from June 1 to September 15, as well as on all Sundays throughout the year.

HUNTING: For deer, small game, and waterfowl.

WINTER ACTIVITIES: Cross-country skiing on all trails on Sunday.

> **For additional information:**
> New Jersey Division of Fish and Wildlife
> Trenton Office
> 501 E. State Street, P.O. Box 400
> Trenton, NJ 08625–0400
> Telephone: (609) 984-0547

Manasquan Reservoir

Howell Township, Monmouth County • *1,204 acres*

LOCATION: Take the Garden State Parkway to exit 98, I–195 west. Proceed on I–195 west to exit 28B, Route 9 (North Freehold). Stay in the right lane when entering Route 9 north. At the first traffic light, turn right onto Georgia Tavern Road. Follow Georgia Tavern Road for 0.3 miles. Turn right onto Windeler Road. Continue 1.5 miles to the Reservoir Area on the left.

HOURS: The grounds are open from dawn to dusk. The Environmental Center is open daily, from 10:00 A.M. to 5:00 P.M., and Friday evenings until 8:30 P.M. The Visitor Center is open daily, from 6:00 A.M. to 8:00 P.M.

ENTRANCE FEE: None.

HANDICAP ACCESS: The Environmental Center is handicap accessible.

SPECIAL FEATURES

Manasquan Reservoir Environmental Center—Exhibits, displays, live animals, and information. For more information, call (732) 751-9453; or visit http://www.monmouthcountyparks.com/parks/mrec.htm.

Visitor Center—Bait shop, vending machines, and boat rental. For more information, call (732) 919-0996.

PICNICKING: Two areas, with a playground and a restroom nearby. No fires.

BOATING: A boat ramp is open daily, March 1 through October 31. Boat rentals are available (kayaks and rowboats with motors). All private boats must have a permit issued by the Monmouth County Park System. Electric motors only.

FISHING: Excellent fishing for bass in the 720-acre reservoir. It is also stocked with trout.

HIKING: More than five miles of marked trails.

MOUNTAIN BIKING: Permitted on the trails.

HORSEBACK RIDING: Permitted on the trails.

WINTER ACTIVITIES: Cross-country skiing, ice skating, and ice fishing.

Manasquan Reservoir.

For additional information:
Monmouth County Park System
805 Newman Springs Road
Lincroft, NJ 07738
Telephone: (732) 842-4000

 Manasquan River
Wildlife Management Area

Ramshorn Drive • Brick and Wall Townships •
744 acres

LOCATION: Located east of the Garden State Parkway, north of Route 549 (Herbertsville Road), and south of Allenwood. River access is from Ramshorn Drive.

HOURS: Dawn to dusk.

ENTRANCE FEE: None.

HANDICAP ACCESS: None.

BOATING: Car-top boat launch.

FISHING: Permitted in the Manasquan River, which is stocked with trout.

HIKING: Informal trails.

MOUNTAIN BIKING: Allowed on existing trails and secondary roads from March 1 to April 15, and from June 1 to September 15, as well as on all Sundays throughout the year.

HUNTING: For deer, small game, and waterfowl.

WINTER ACTIVITIES: Cross-country skiing on all trails on Sunday.

For additional information:
New Jersey Division of Fish and Wildlife
Trenton Office
501 E. State Street, P.O. Box 400
Trenton, NJ 08625–0400
Telephone: (609) 984-0547

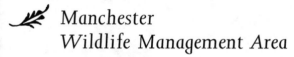 Manchester
Wildlife Management Area

Horicon Road, Manchester Township ♦ 3,085 acres

LOCATION: Off Route 539, north of Route 70 and the town of Whiting.

HOURS: Dawn to dusk.

ENTRANCE FEE: None.

HANDICAP ACCESS: None.

HIKING: Informal trails.

MOUNTAIN BIKING: Allowed on existing trails and secondary roads from March 1 to April 15, and from June 1 to September 15, as well as on all Sundays throughout the year.

HUNTING: For deer, small game, and turkey.

WINTER ACTIVITIES: Cross-country skiing on all trails on Sunday.

For additional information:
New Jersey Division of Fish and Wildlife
Trenton Office
501 E. State Street, P.O. Box 400
Trenton, NJ 08625–0400
Telephone: (609) 984-0547

Manchester Wildlife Management Area.

Michael Brown

Monmouth Battlefield State Park

Route 33, Manalapan • *2,366 acres*

LOCATION: North of Route 33, between Routes 9 and 527. Craig House is located on Schibanoff Road, off Route 9.

HOURS: The grounds are open from dawn to dusk. The Visitor Center is open during the summer, from 9:00 A.M. to 5:00 P.M., and during the winter, from 9:00 A.M. to 4:00 P.M. Craig House is open during the summer, Wednesdays and Sundays, from 9:00 A.M. to 4:00 P.M., and during the winter by appointment only.

ENTRANCE FEE: None.

HANDICAP ACCESS: The Visitor Center, Craig House, and the picnic areas and restrooms are handicap accessible.

SPECIAL FEATURES

Craig House—During the battle, this farmhouse was the home of John and Ann Craig and their three children. The 1746 kitchen is Dutch framed, while the two-story addition is English framed. The Friends of Monmouth Battlefield provide guided tours of the refurnished house at specific times.

Visitor Center—Features exhibits and artifacts from the Battle of Monmouth and also from the Civil War. For more information, call (732)780-5782.

PICNICKING: Open and lightly wooded areas, with grills, a playground, and restrooms.

FISHING: For children, at the pond at Liberty Grove picnic area.

HIKING: Twenty-five miles of marked and unmarked trails. A trail map is available at the Nature Center.

MOUNTAIN BIKING: Permitted on trails.

HUNTING: Permitted in designated areas (1,244 acres), for deer, by special permit only.

WINTER ACTIVITIES: Cross-country skiing and sledding.

For additional information:
347 Freehold-Englishtown Road
Manalapan, NJ 07726
Telephone: (732) 462-9616; Fax: (732) 577-8816

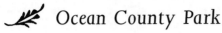

Ocean County Park

Ocean Avenue (Route 88) ◆ *Lakewood Township,*
Ocean County ◆ *326 acres*

LOCATION: Access is from Route 88 (Ocean Avenue), just east of Lakewood. From the Garden State Parkway southbound, take exit 91 (Route 549/Lanes Mill Road) south to Route 88. Travel west on Route 88, about 2 miles, to the park entrance on the right. From the Garden State Parkway northbound, take exit 90 (Route 549/Chambers Bridge Road), to the jug handle for the U-turn. Go north for about 0.5 miles to Route 88. Travel west on Route 88 for about 2 miles, to the park entrance on the right.

HOURS: Dawn to dusk.

ENTRANCE FEE: No fee.

HANDICAP ACCESS: The picnic facilities are handicap accessible.

PICNICKING: Large wooded picnic area around Duck Lake (last parking area before the park exit) that has a playground and restrooms.

FISHING: There are three lakes for fishing. Lake Fishgan, the southernmost lake, is for children only (fourteen and younger).

SWIMMING: The beach complex is located at the northernmost lake (the first parking area). Lifeguards are on duty from 10:00 A.M. to 6:00 P.M. A playground and restrooms are nearby.

For additional information:
Ocean County Parks and Recreation Department
1198 Brandon Road
Toms River, NJ 08753
Telephone: (732) 506-9090

Poricy Park

Oak Hill Road ◆ *Middletown, Monmouth County* ◆
250 acres

LOCATION: Located just west of Route 35, in Middletown.

HOURS: The grounds are open from dawn to dusk. The Nature Center is open, Monday through Friday, from 9:00 A.M. to 4:00 P.M., and on Sunday, from 12:30 P.M. to 3:30 P.M. The farmhouse is open the last Sunday of the month, from 1:00 P.M. to 3:00 P.M.

ENTRANCE FEE: None.

HANDICAP ACCESS: The Nature Center and the restrooms are handicap accessible.

SPECIAL FEATURES

Murray Farmhouse—Eighteenth-century farmhouse and barn still on the original foundations and in the original setting.

Poricy Brook Fossil Beds—These fossil beds are well known to collectors in the northeast. No charge for groups of less than ten. Call the Nature Center for details.

Poricy Park Nature Center—Information and displays, as well as live animals.

HIKING: Marked trails.

For additional information:
Poricy Park Nature Center
Oak Hill Road, P.O. Box 36
Middletown, NJ 07748
Telephone: (732) 842-5966; Fax: (732) 842-6833

 # Prospertown Lake
Wildlife Management Area

Route 537 • Jackson Township, Ocean County •
130 acres

LOCATION: Off Route 537, northeast of Prospertown.

HOURS: Dawn to dusk.

ENTRANCE FEE: None.

HANDICAP ACCESS: A fishing pier is available for disabled people in wheelchairs.

BOATING: Permitted for car-top boats only. No motors. There is no ramp on the lake.

FISHING: Permitted in the 80-acre lake, which is stocked during the trout season, primarily with brown trout. Bank fishing is permitted on approximately fifteen percent of the shore.

Michael Brown

Prospertown Lake, Prospertown Wildlife Management Area.

For additional information:
New Jersey Division of Fish and Wildlife
Trenton Office
501 E. State Street, P.O. Box 400
Trenton, NJ 08625—0400
Telephone: (609) 984-0547

 Sedge Islands Wildlife Management Area

Ocean Township, Ocean County ◆ 192 acres

LOCATION: Off the southwestern end of Island Beach State Park. Access is by boat only.

HOURS: Dawn to dusk.

ENTRANCE FEE: None.

HANDICAP ACCESS: None.

FISHING: Permitted in the ocean and in the channels around the islands.

CRABBING: Permitted in the ocean and in the channels around the islands.

HUNTING: For waterfowl.

For additional information:
New Jersey Division of Fish and Wildlife
Trenton Office
501 E. State Street, P.O. Box 400
Trenton, NJ 08625–0400
Telephone: (609) 984-0547

 # Seven Presidents Oceanfront Park

Ocean Avenue • Long Branch, Monmouth County • 38 acres

LOCATION: Off Route 36, on the shore, north of Route 537.

HOURS: Open from 8:00 A.M. to dusk.

ENTRANCE FEE: Parking and admission fee charged from Memorial Day weekend to Labor Day.

HANDICAP ACCESS: There are beach wheelchairs available.

DESCRIPTION: This park commemorates the seven United States presidents who regularly vacationed at the New Jersey shore.

PICNICKING: Tables, no grills, with a playground and restrooms nearby.

BOATING: A boat ramp is available for trailer and car-top boats.

FISHING: Permitted away from the swimming area.

SWIMMING: Lifeguard-supervised ocean swimming is offered at the 4,700-foot-long beach during the summer. Modern restrooms and changing rooms are provided, and a food concession is open from Memorial Day weekend to Labor Day.

For additional information:
Monmouth County Park System
805 Newman Springs Road
Lincroft, NJ 07738
Telephone: (732) 842-4000

 # Shark River Park

School House Road • Neptune, Monmouth County • 587 acres

LOCATION: South of Route 33, and west of Route 18.

HOURS: Dawn to dusk.

ENTRANCE FEE: None.

HANDICAP ACCESS: None.

PICNICKING: Tables, with a playground and restrooms.

FISHING: Permitted in the 3-acre lake, and in the Shark River.

HIKING: Several marked trails of varying length.

WINTER ACTIVITIES: Cross-country skiing and ice skating.

For additional information:
Monmouth County Park System
805 Newman Springs Road
Lincroft, NJ 07738
Telephone: (732) 842-4000

Stafford Forge
Wildlife Management Area

Route 539 • Eagleswood and Little Egg Harbor Townships •
Ocean County • 15,352 acres

LOCATION: West of the Garden State Parkway, near Stafford Forge. Route 539 runs through part of the area.

HOURS: Dawn to dusk.

ENTRANCE FEE: None.

HANDICAP ACCESS: None.

BOATING: Allowed in the ponds (68, 73, 48, and 22 acres). Car-top boat launch.

FISHING: Permitted in the four ponds.

HIKING: Informal trails.

MOUNTAIN BIKING: Allowed on existing trails and secondary roads from March 1 to April 15, and from June 1 to September 15, as well as on all Sundays throughout the year.

HUNTING: For deer, small game, turkey, and waterfowl.

WINTER ACTIVITIES: Cross-country skiing on all trails on Sunday.

For additional information:
New Jersey Division of Fish and Wildlife
Trenton Office
501 E. State Street P.O. Box 400
Trenton, NJ 08625–0400
Telephone: (609) 984-0547

Stanley "Tip" Seaman County Park

120 Lakeside Drive (Route 9) • *Tuckerton, Ocean County* •
22 acres

LOCATION: Off Route 9 (West Main Street) in Tuckerton, and west of
Route 539. Take the Garden State Parkway, exit 58. Travel east on
Route 539 (Green Street), about 5 miles, and turn right on Route
9S. The park entrance is about 0.25 miles on the right, past Lake
Pohatcong.

HOURS: The grounds are open from dawn to dusk; the office is open,
Monday through Friday, from 8:00 A.M. to 3:30 P.M.

ENTRANCE FEE: None.

HANDICAP ACCESS: The office, restrooms, and picnic area are handicap
accessible.

PICNICKING: Available, with a restroom and a playground.

FISHING: Permitted in 33-acre Lake Pohatcong.

For additional information:

Ocean County Parks and Recreation Department
1198 Brandon Road
Toms River, NJ 08753
Telephone: (732) 506-9090

 # Tatum Park

Red Hill Road • *Middletown, Monmouth County* •
368 acres

LOCATION: Northeast of the Garden State Parkway, exit 114, and across
from Deer Cut Park.

HOURS: Dawn to dusk.

ENTRANCE FEE: None.

HANDICAP ACCESS: The picnic area is handicap accessible.

PICNICKING: Two areas, with tables and a restroom nearby. One area has
a playground.

HIKING: Several marked trails, totaling more than four miles.

MOUNTAIN BIKING: Permitted on some trails.

HORSEBACK RIDING: Permitted on some trails.

WINTER ACTIVITIES: Cross-country skiing.

For additional information:
Monmouth County Park System
805 Newman Springs Road
Lincroft, NJ 07738
Telephone: (732) 842-4000

 # Thompson Park

Newman Springs Road ♦ *Lincroft, Monmouth County* ♦
665 acres

LOCATION: Off Route 520 (Newman Springs Road), west of the Garden State Parkway, exit 109. Backs up to Swimming River Reservoir.

HOURS: The grounds are open from 8:00 A.M. to dusk; the park office is open, Monday through Friday, from 8:00 A.M. to 4:30 P.M.

ENTRANCE FEE: None.

HANDICAP ACCESS: The picnic area is handicap accessible.

PICNICKING: Tables with grills, with a playground and restrooms.

BOATING: Trailer and car-top boat launch. No gas motors.

Thompson Park.

Monmouth County Park System

FISHING: Excellent fishing for bass in the 22-acre lake.

HIKING: Several marked trails.

WINTER ACTIVITIES: Cross-country skiing.

> **For additional information:**
> Monmouth County Park System
> 805 Newman Springs Road
> Lincroft, NJ 07738
> Telephone: (732) 842-4000

 Turkey Swamp Park

Georgia Road • Freehold Township, Monmouth County •
1,300 acres

LOCATION: From I–195, take exit 22. Turn north onto Jackson Mills Road, then west onto Georgia Road.

HOURS: The grounds are open from dawn to dusk. The campground office is open daily, from 9:00 A.M. to 10:00 P.M., during the camping season.

ENTRANCE FEE: None.

HANDICAP ACCESS: The campsite, the ramp to the fishing and boating area, the picnic area, and restrooms are handicap accessible.

CAMPING: Sixty-four sites for tents and trailers are available from March 15 to November 30. Every site has water and electric hookups. Modern restrooms are available, with hot showers and laundry. A playground is also located near the campground. For more information, call the campground office, (732) 462-7286.

PICNICKING: Tables with grills, a playground, and restrooms.

BOATING: Allowed on the 17-acre lake. Canoes, rowboats, kayaks, and paddle boats can be rented during the summer season, daily, from 10:00 A.M. to 4:30 P.M.

FISHING: Permitted in the lake.

HIKING: More than four miles of marked trails.

MOUNTAIN BIKING: Permitted on trails.

HORSEBACK RIDING: Permitted on trails.

WINTER ACTIVITIES: Cross-country skiing and ice skating.

Turkey Swamp Park.

For additional information:
Monmouth County Park System
805 Newman Springs Road
Lincroft, NJ 07738
Telephone: (732) 842-4000

 Turkey Swamp
Wildlife Management Area

Freehold Township, Monmouth County ◆ 2,693 acres

LOCATION: East of Route 527, and north of I–195, exit 21.

HOURS: Dawn to dusk.

ENTRANCE FEE: None.

HANDICAP ACCESS: None.

HIKING: Informal trails.

MOUNTAIN BIKING: Allowed on existing trails and secondary roads from March 1 to April 15, and from June 1 to September 15, as well as on all Sundays throughout the year.

HUNTING: For deer and small game.

WINTER ACTIVITIES: Cross-country skiing on all trails on Sunday.

For additional information:
New Jersey Division of Fish and Wildlife
Trenton Office
501 E. State Street, P.O. Box 400
Trenton, NJ 08625–0400
Telephone: (609) 984-0547

Upper Barnegat Bay Wildlife Management Area

Ocean County ♦ 174 acres

LOCATION: West of Route 35, between the towns of Normandy Beach and Lavallette.

HOURS: Dawn to dusk.

ENTRANCE FEE: None.

HANDICAP ACCESS: None.

BOATING: Allowed in the bay.

FISHING: Permitted in the bay.

CRABBING: Permitted in the bay.

HUNTING: For waterfowl.

For additional information:
New Jersey Division of Fish and Wildlife
Trenton Office
501 E. State Street, P.O. Box 400
Trenton, NJ 08625–0400
Telephone: (609) 984-0547

Wells Mills County Park

Route 532 ♦ Waretown, Ocean County ♦ 910 acres

LOCATION: South of Route 532 (Wells Mills Road), and west of the Garden State Parkway, exit 69. From the Garden State Parkway northbound, take exit 69 (Route 532). Turn left (west), and proceed 2.5 miles, to the park entrance on the left. From the Garden State Parkway southbound, take exit 67 (Barnegat, Chatsworth). Turn right on West Bay Avenue (Route 554). Travel for about 5 miles to Route 72. Take Route 72 west a short distance, to Route 532 east. Turn right, and proceed 3.8 miles to the park entrance on the right.

HOURS: The grounds are open from dawn to dusk. The Nature Center is open weekdays, from 10:00 A.M. to 4:00 P.M., and weekends, from 10:00 A.M. to 6:00 P.M.

ENTRANCE FEE: No fee.

HANDICAP ACCESS: There is a trail for the visually impaired.

SPECIAL FEATURES
Nature Center—Displays and exhibits of nature and of the history of the Pinelands, as well as live animals. For more information, call (609) 971-3085.

PICNICKING: Tables with grills, with a play area and restrooms.

BOATING: Car-top boat launch on 34-acre lake. Canoe rentals available.

FISHING: Permitted in the lake, with fishing dock.

HIKING: Extensive network of marked trails.

> **For additional information:**
> *Ocean County Parks and Recreation Department*
> *1198 Brandon Road*
> *Toms River, NJ 08753*
> *Telephone: (732) 506-9090*

 ## Whiting Wildlife Management Area

Ocean County • 1,191 acres

LOCATION: South of Route 70, near the town of Whiting.

HOURS: Dawn to dusk

ENTRANCE FEE: None.

HANDICAP ACCESS: None.

FISHING: Limited fishing in small pond.

HIKING: Informal trails.

MOUNTAIN BIKING: Allowed on existing trails and secondary roads from March 1 to April 15, and from June 1 to September 15, as well as on all Sundays throughout the year.

HUNTING: For deer, small game, and turkey.

WINTER ACTIVITIES: Cross-country skiing on all trails on Sunday.

For additional information:

New Jersey Division of Fish and Wildlife
Trenton Office
501 E. State Street, P.O. Box 400
Trenton, NJ 08625–0400
Telephone: (609) 984-0547

Region Five

Burlington, Camden,
Gloucester, & Salem Counties

Roger R. Locandro

Blueberries, Port Republic.

BURLINGTON

BORDENTOWN

545

295

537

130

CAMDEN

24

MOUNT HOLLY

BROWNS MILLS

530

CAMDEN

5

18

22

4

20 16

13

11

73

MEDFORD LAKES

72

25

541

WOODBURY

10

3

534

23

6

553

BERLIN

31

295

536

14

42

19

BATSTO

563

GLASSBORO

9

33

NEW GRETNA

26

12

27

WILLIAMS TOWN

542

2

45

WOODSTOWN

555

32

29

8

581

GLOUCESTER

28

SALEM

7

ALLOWAY

1

30

49

17

21

15

SALEM

0   5
miles

Parks

•   Selected Towns

    Selected Roads

    County Borders

Mike Siegel, Rutgers Cartography

198

1 Abbotts Meadow Wildlife Management Area
2 Bass River State Forest
3 Berlin Park
4 Brendan T. Byrne State Forest
5 Cooper River Park
6 D.O.D. Ponds Wildlife Management Area
7 Elmer Lake Wildlife Management Area
8 Fort Mott State Park
9 Glassboro Wildlife Management Area
10 Greenwich Lake Park
11 Haddon Lake Park
12 Harrisonville Lake Wildlife Management Area
13 Hopkins Pond
14 James G. Atkinson Memorial Park
15 Mad Horse Creek Wildlife Management Area
16 Maria Barnaby Greenwald Memorial Park
17 Maskells Mill Pond Wildlife Management Area
18 Medford Wildlife Management Area
19 New Brooklyn Park
20 Newton Lake Park
21 Parvin State Park
22 Pemberton Lake Wildlife Management Area
23 Penn State Forest
24 Rancocas State Park
25 Red Bank Battlefield Park
26 Salem River Wildlife Management Area
27 Scotland Run Park
28 Supawna Meadows National Wildlife Refuge
29 Swan Bay Wildlife Management Area
30 Thundergust Pond Wildlife Management Area
31 Wharton State Forest
32 White Oak Branch Wildlife Management Area
33 Winslow Wildlife Management Area

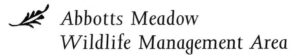

Abbotts Meadow
Wildlife Management Area

Salem County • *975 acres*

LOCATION: Located west of Route 49, near Hancocks Bridge.

HOURS: Dawn to dusk.

ENTRANCE FEE: None.

HANDICAP ACCESS: None.

HIKING: Informal trails.

MOUNTAIN BIKING: Allowed on existing trails and secondary roads on wildlife management areas from March 1 to April 15, and from June 1 to September 15, as well as on all Sundays throughout the year.

HORSEBACK RIDING: Allowed on all trails, with permit.

HUNTING: For deer, small game, and waterfowl.

WINTER ACTIVITIES: Cross-country skiing can be enjoyed on all of the trails in the tract on Sunday.

> **For additional information:**
> *New Jersey Division of Fish and Wildlife*
> *Trenton Office*
> *501 E. State Street, P.O. Box 400*
> *Trenton, NJ 08625–0400*
> *Telephone: (609) 984-0547*

 # Bass River State Forest

Stage Road, Burlington County • *New Gretna* • *26,439 acres*

LOCATION: Access is from the Garden State Parkway, exit 52 south, and from exit 50 north. Follow brown forest signs.

HOURS: The grounds are open from 8:00 A.M. to 8:00 P.M. The park office is open daily, from 8:00 A.M. to 4:30 P.M., later on weekends from Memorial Day weekend through Labor Day. The boat concession is open, Memorial Day to late June, from 10:00 A.M. to 5:30 P.M. on weekends, and daily from late June to Labor Day.

ENTRANCE FEE: Fee charged from Memorial Day weekend to Labor Day.

HANDICAP ACCESS: Several picnic tables at the beach area are wheelchair accessible, and four campsites adjacent to the shower/restroom buildings are designated handicap accessible.

SPECIAL FEATURES

West Pine Plains Natural Area—Consists of 3,830 acres designed to preserve a significant portion of the globally rare pine plains community. Known to occur only in areas of New Jersey and New York, it is characterized by a naturally stunted forest.

Nature Center—Located in the south shore camping area, the Nature Center serves as a resource for nature study. Open Memorial Day weekend through Labor Day. Call for hours.

CABINS: Six cabins are located along the north shore of Lake Absegami. Each is designed to accommodate six people. Cabins come with two bunk rooms, a living room, a kitchen (with electric stove and refrigerator), and an enclosed porch. The bathroom includes a shower, hot water, and a toilet. Cabins are closed from November 1 to March 31.

SHELTERS: Six shelters are located along the north shore of the lake and are designed to accommodate four people. There is no running water or electricity, although drinking water, showers, and flush toilets are within walking distance. Each has two bunk rooms and a small living room. Shelters are closed from November 1 to March 31.

LEAN-TOS: Nine fully enclosed lean-tos are situated along the lake for year-round camping. Each consists of one unfurnished room, accommodating up to six people. There is a small stove for heating. Each site has a picnic table and charcoal grill. Within walking distance are drinking water, showers, and flush toilets. A nonflush, handicap-accessible restroom is located in the lean-to area.

CAMPING: Near the lake, in a wooded area, are 175 family campsites. Each site has a picnic table and fire ring. Dumping stations are located nearby for trailers; no water, electric, or sewer connections are available.

PICNICKING: Large, lightly shaded area with tables and grills, adjoining the beach area.

BOATING: A rowboat concession is open during the summer.

FISHING: Permitted in the lake, away from the swimming area. Pickerel, sunfish, and catfish are the main species found in the lake, but they are not plentiful.

SWIMMING: On the eastern shore of 67-acre Lake Absegami. There is a beach with lifeguard supervision during the summer. Nearby are parking areas, a bathhouse, first aid, a concession stand, and a playground.

HIKING: Many miles of sand and gravel roads are open for year-round hiking. There is also a one-half mile self-guided nature trail.

MOUNTAIN BIKING: Permitted on the sand roads.

HORSEBACK RIDING: Permitted on the sand roads.

HUNTING: Permitted in designated areas (26,000 acres), for deer, small game, and turkey.

WINTER ACTIVITIES: Cross-country skiing.

For additional information:
762 Stage Road
P.O. Box 118
New Gretna, NJ 08224
Telephone: (609) 296-1114

 # Berlin Park

Park Drive • Berlin, Camden County • 152 acres

LOCATION: Located in Berlin, between the White Horse Pike, New Freedom Road, and Park Drive.

HOURS: The grounds are open from 6:00 A.M. to 10:00 P.M. Call the Environmental Studies Center for hours.

ENTRANCE FEE: None.

HANDICAP ACCESS: The Environmental Center, picnic areas, and playgrounds are handicap accessible.

SPECIAL FEATURES
Camden County Environmental Studies Center—Educational programs and informational services. For more information, call (856) 768-1598.

PICNICKING: Throughout the park, with tables, grills, a playground, and portable toilets in the spring and summer.

FISHING: Permitted in the Great Egg Harbor River.

HIKING: Five miles of nature trails.

For additional information:
Camden County Department of Parks
1301 Park Boulevard
Cherry Hill, NJ 08002–3752
Telephone: (856) 216-2117

 # Brendan T. Byrne State Forest

Route 72 ♦ 34,725 acres

LOCATION: The park entrance is 1 mile southeast of the intersection of Routes 70 and 72.

HOURS: The grounds are open from dawn to dusk. The park office is open daily, year-round, from 8:00 A.M. to 4:30 P.M., later on Friday and Saturday evenings from Memorial Day weekend through Labor Day. The Sawmill Interpretive Center is open Memorial Day weekend to Labor Day, Wednesday through Sunday, from 8:00 A.M. to 4:30 P.M. Hours may vary.

ENTRANCE FEE: None.

HANDICAP ACCESS: Cranberry Trail is handicap accessible. Yurts are also accessible.

SPECIAL FEATURES

Whitesbog Village—Nineteenth- and early twentieth-century cranberry and blueberry producing village undergoing restoration. Call (609) 893-4646 for tours and additional information.

Sawmill Interpretive Center—Exhibits, displays, park information, and summer programs.

CABINS: Three cabins are situated in a wooded area adjacent to Pakim Pond. They are available for weekly rentals from April 1 through October 31. Each cabin, accommodating four people, has a main room with a fireplace, two double-deck bunks, a table, and benches. The kitchen has running water, an electric range, an oven, and a refrigerator. There is also a toilet and basin. Showers are available at the camp area restroom.

YURTS: There are three yurts: circular tents built on a wood frame, featuring wood floors, a deck, and a Plexiglas skylight. Each yurt has a lockable wood door, window screens and flaps, and two double-deck bunks, which sleep up to four people. Accessible to people with disabilities. Convenient to restroom with hot showers.

CAMPING: Eighty-two sites are available all year. Each site has a table and grill. Modern restrooms, showers, and laundry facilities are available, and a playground is nearby.

PICNICKING: Tables with grills, and a restroom, are located at Pakim Pond Recreational Area.

FISHING: Although fish are not plentiful, fishing is allowed at Pakim Pond, and also in streams throughout the forest.

HIKING: There are more than 100 miles of unmarked sand and gravel roads throughout the forest. The Batona Trail, a marked 49.5-mile trail, starts in Brendan T. Byrne State Forest and continues for 9.4 miles before going on to Wharton State Forest. Trail maps are available at the park office.

MOUNTAIN BIKING: Permitted on some trails.

HORSEBACK RIDING: Permitted on the miles of sand roads.

HUNTING: Permitted in designated areas (30,310 acres), for deer, small game, turkey, and waterfowl.

WINTER ACTIVITIES: Cross-country skiing.

For additional information:
P.O. Box 215
New Lisbon, NJ 08064
Telephone: (609) 726-1191

Cooper River Park

Cherry Hill, Pennsauken, and Collingswood and Haddon Townships ◆ *Camden County* ◆ *347 acres*

LOCATION: This linear park is bounded by North and South Park Drives, Route 130, and Grove Street.

HOURS: The grounds are open from 6:00 A.M. to 10:00 P.M.; the stadium area is open until midnight.

ENTRANCE FEE: None.

HANDICAP ACCESS: An indoor restroom, some picnic areas, and a playground are handicap accessible.

Cooper River Park. Camden County Park System.

PICNICKING: Several picnic areas are situated around the park, one with a large playground and seasonal toilets.

BOATING: Allowed in the Cooper River. A boat ramp is located on South Park Drive and is suitable for trailer and car-top boats. No gas motors.

FISHING: Permitted in the Cooper River.

HIKING: There are several pathways in the park.

WINTER ACTIVITIES: Cross-country skiing.

> **For additional information:**
> Camden County Department of Parks
> 1301 Park Boulevard
> Cherry Hill, NJ 08002–3752
> Telephone: (856) 216-2117

 # D.O.D. Ponds Wildlife Management Area

Salem County ◆ 336 acres

LOCATION: Located west of Route 130, and north of the town of Penns Grove.

HOURS: Dawn to dusk.

ENTRANCE FEE: None.

HANDICAP ACCESS: None.

BOATING: Car-top boat launch and ramp at 120-acre D.O.D. Lake.

FISHING: Permitted in the lake.

HUNTING: For small game and waterfowl.

> **For additional information:**
> New Jersey Division of Fish and Wildlife
> Trenton Office
> 501 E. State Street, P.O. Box 400
> Trenton, NJ 08625–0400
> Telephone: (609) 984-0547

Elmer Lake Wildlife Management Area

Salem County ◆ 279 acres

LOCATION: Bisected by Route 40, near the town of Elmer.

HOURS: Dawn to dusk.

ENTRANCE FEE: None.

HANDICAP ACCESS: None.

BOATING: Car-top boat launch and ramp at 45-acre Elmer Lake.

FISHING: Permitted in the lake.

HUNTING: For deer, small game, and waterfowl.

> **For additional information:**
> New Jersey Division of Fish and Wildlife
> Trenton Office
> 501 E. State Street, P.O. Box 400
> Trenton, NJ 08625–0400
> Telephone: (609) 984-0547

Fort Mott State Park

Fort Mott Road ◆ Pennsville, Salem County ◆ 104 acres

LOCATION: Located west of Route 49, and 6 miles south of the Delaware Memorial Bridge in Salem County.

HOURS: The grounds are open from dawn to dusk. The park office is open daily, Memorial Day weekend through Labor Day, from 8:00

Greg Johnson

Fort Mott State Park.

A.M. to 8:30 P.M.; during the rest of the year, it is open daily, from 8:00 A.M. to 4:30 P.M.

ENTRANCE FEE: None.

HANDICAP ACCESS: The picnic area and restrooms are handicap accessible.

Fort Mott State Park.

Bruce E. Mathews

DESCRIPTION: Begun in 1896 and finished one year later, the fort is named in honor of Major General Gershom Mott, a decorated Civil War veteran and native of New Jersey. After World War II, the fort was decommissioned, and the armament removed. In 1947, the state acquired the land.

SPECIAL FEATURES

Fort Mott—Designed originally as part of a three-fort defense system for the Delaware River.

PICNICKING: Large, open picnic area with grills, a playground, water, and restrooms.

FISHING: Permitted in the Delaware River.

Glassboro Wildlife Management Area

Glassboro and Clayton Townships • 2,368 acres

LOCATION: Located east of Route 47 (Delsea Drive), and south of Route 322, northeast of Clayton.

HOURS: Dawn to dusk.

ENTRANCE FEE: None.

HANDICAP ACCESS: None.

HIKING: Informal trails.

MOUNTAIN BIKING: Allowed on existing trails and secondary roads on wildlife management areas from March 1 to April 15, and from June 1 to September 15, as well as on all Sundays throughout the year.

HORSEBACK RIDING: Allowed on all trails, with a permit.

HUNTING: For deer, small game, and turkey.

WINTER ACTIVITIES: Cross-country skiing can be enjoyed on all of the trails in the tract on Sunday.

> **For additional information:**
> New Jersey Division of Fish and Wildlife
> Trenton Office
> 501 E. State Street, P.O. Box 400
> Trenton, NJ 08625–0400
> Telephone: (609) 984-0547

Greenwich Lake Park

Tomlin Station Road • Gibbstown • 80 acres

LOCATION: Off I–295 south, at exit 15.

HOURS: Dawn to dusk.

ENTRANCE FEE: None.

HANDICAP ACCESS: The picnic area and restrooms are handicap accessible.

PICNICKING: Tables with grills, with a playground and restrooms.

BOATING: Car-top boat launch is available daily, from Memorial Day weekend to Labor Day.

FISHING: Permitted in 40-acre Greenwich Lake.

> **For additional information:**
> Gloucester County Parks & Recreation
> 6 Blackwell-Barnsboro Road
> Sewell, NJ 08080
> Telephone: (609) 468-0100; Fax: (609) 468-4497

Haddon Lake Park

Haddon Heights, and Audubon and Mt. Ephraim Townships ◆ *Camden County* ◆ *79 acres*

LOCATION: This linear park runs from Station Avenue to the Black Horse Pike, north of Route 551, and east of Route 168.

HOURS: Dawn to dusk.

ENTRANCE FEE: None.

HANDICAP ACCESS: The fishing piers, picnic areas, and playgrounds are handicap accessible.

PICNICKING: Tables with grills, with playgrounds and seasonal toilets.

BOATING: Car-top boat launch for nonmotorized small boats.

FISHING: Permitted in 11-acre Haddon Lake, which is stocked with trout. A fishing pier is located at the lake.

WINTER ACTIVITIES: Cross-country skiing.

> **For additional information:**
> Camden County Department of Parks
> 1301 Park Blvd.
> Cherry Hill, NJ 08002–3752
> Telephone: (856) 216-2117

Harrisonville Lake
Wildlife Management Area

Gloucester and Salem Counties ◆ *37 acres*

LOCATION: On the county line, east of Route 45, and south of Harrisonville.

Harrisonville Lake Wildlife Management Area.

HOURS: Dawn to dusk.

ENTRANCE FEE: None.

HANDICAP ACCESS: None.

BOATING: Allowed on the 30-acre lake. Car-top boats only. No gas motors.

FISHING: Permitted in the lake, which is stocked with trout. Bank fishing is also possible on a portion of the shoreline.

For additional information:
New Jersey Division of Fish and Wildlife
Trenton Office
501 E. State Street, P.O. Box 400
Trenton, NJ 08625–0400
Telephone: (609) 984-0547

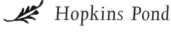 Hopkins Pond

Hopkins Lane ♦ Haddonfield, Camden County ♦ 33 acres

LOCATION: In Haddonfield, off Grove Street, on both sides of Hopkins Lane.

HOURS: Open from 6:00 A.M. to 10:00 P.M.

ENTRANCE FEE: None.

HANDICAP ACCESS: None.

FISHING: Permitted in 5-acre pond.

HIKING: An 0.6-mile, self-guided tree-identification trail leads around the pond. A brochure is available at the park's administration building.

> **For additional information:**
> Camden County Department of Parks
> 1301 Park Boulevard
> Cherry Hill, NJ 08002–3752
> Telephone: (856) 216-2117

 # James G. Atkinson Memorial Park

Delsea Drive and Bethel Mill Road ◆ Hurffville ◆ 60 acres

LOCATION: Off Route 47, just east of Pitman.

HOURS: Dawn to dusk.

ENTRANCE FEE: None.

HANDICAP ACCESS: The picnic area and restrooms are handicap accessible.

PICNICKING: Tables with grills, with a playground and a restroom.

> **For additional information:**
> Gloucester County Parks and Recreation
> 6 Blackwell-Barnsboro Road
> Sewell, NJ 08080
> Telephone: (609) 468-0100; Fax: (609) 468-4497

 # Mad Horse Creek
Wildlife Management Area

Lower Alloways Creek Township ◆ Salem County ◆ 8,477 acres

LOCATION: Located southwest of Canton, on the Delaware Bay.

HOURS: Dawn to dusk.

ENTRANCE FEE: None.

HANDICAP ACCESS: None.

BOATING: A boat ramp is available that provides access to the tract, and to the Delaware Bay.

FISHING: Good saltwater fishing in the streams and creeks within the tract, and in the bay. The main species are white perch and striped bass.

CRABBING: Permitted in the streams, creeks, and bay.

HUNTING: For deer, small game, turkey, and waterfowl.

For additional information:
New Jersey Division of Fish and Wildlife
Trenton Office
501 E. State Street, P.O. Box 400
Trenton, NJ 08625–0400
Telephone: (609) 984-0547

Maria Barnaby Greenwald Memorial Park

Park Boulevard ◆ Cherry Hill, Camden County ◆ 47 acres

LOCATION: Bounded by Kings Highway, Park Boulevard, and Grove Street.

HOURS: Open from 6:00 A.M. to 10:00 P.M.

ENTRANCE FEE: None.

HANDICAP ACCESS: None.

FISHING: Permitted in Driscoll Pond.

HIKING: There is a 1.8-mile wildlife-viewing trail.

WINTER ACTIVITIES: Cross-country skiing.

For additional information:
Camden County Department of Parks
1301 Park Boulevard
Cherry Hill, NJ 08002–3752
Telephone: (856) 216-2117

Maskells Mill Pond Wildlife Management Area

Salem County ◆ 612 acres

HOURS: Dawn to dusk.

LOCATION: Located west of Route 49, near the town of Harmersville.

ENTRANCE FEE: None.

HANDICAP ACCESS: None.

BOATING: Allowed in 33-acre Maskells Mill Pond; small craft only.

FISHING: Permitted in the pond.

HIKING: Informal trails and dirt roads.

MOUNTAIN BIKING: Allowed on existing trails and secondary roads on wildlife management areas from March 1 to April 15, and from June 1 to September 15, as well as on all Sundays throughout the year.

HORSEBACK RIDING: Allowed on all trails, with a permit.

HUNTING: For deer, small game, turkey, and waterfowl.

WINTER ACTIVITIES: Cross-country skiing can be enjoyed on all of the trails in the tract on Sunday.

> **For additional information:**
> *New Jersey Division of Fish and Wildlife*
> *Trenton Office*
> *501 E. State Street, P.O. Box 400*
> *Trenton, NJ 08625–0400*
> *Telephone: (609) 984-0547*

 # Medford Wildlife Management Area

Burlington County ♦ *214 acres*

LOCATION: Located north of Route 70, near the town of Medford.

HOURS: Dawn to dusk.

ENTRANCE FEE: None.

HANDICAP ACCESS: None.

HIKING: Informal trails and sand roads.

MOUNTAIN BIKING: Allowed on existing trails and secondary roads on wildlife management areas from March 1 to April 15, and from June 1 to September 15, as well as on all Sundays throughout the year.

HORSEBACK RIDING: Allowed on all trails, with a permit.

HUNTING: For deer, small game, turkey, and waterfowl.

WINTER ACTIVITIES: Cross-country skiing can be enjoyed on all of the trails in the tract on Sunday.

For additional information:
New Jersey Division of Fish and Wildlife
Trenton Office
501 E. State Street, P.O. Box 400
Trenton, NJ 08625—0400
Telephone: (609) 984-0547

 # New Brooklyn Park

Winslow Township, Camden County • *758 acres*

LOCATION: Located in Winslow Township, between New Freedom and New Brooklyn Roads, north of the Atlantic City Expressway, and east of Route 536.

HOURS: Open from 6:00 A.M. to 10:00 P.M.

ENTRANCE FEE: None.

HANDICAP ACCESS: The picnic areas and playgrounds are handicap accessible.

PICNICKING: Two picnic areas with grills, with a nearby playground and seasonal toilets.

BOATING: Allowed in 100-acre New Brooklyn Lake. Canoe launch.

FISHING: Permitted in the lake and in the Great Egg Harbor River.

HIKING: Informal trails and dirt roads.

HORSEBACK RIDING: Permitted on trails.

For additional information:
Camden County Department of Parks
1301 Park Boulevard
Cherry Hill, NJ 08002—3752
Telephone: (856) 216-2117

 # Newton Lake Park

Collingswood, and Oaklyn and Haddon Townships •
Camden County • *103 acres*

LOCATION: This linear park is bounded by Cuthbert Boulevard and the White Horse Pike. The park is east of Route 130, and south of Route 561.

HOURS: Open from 6:00 A.M. to 10:00 P.M.

ENTRANCE FEE: None.

HANDICAP ACCESS: The picnic areas, fishing piers, and playgrounds are handicap accessible.

PICNICKING: Tables throughout the park, with grills, a playground, and seasonal toilets.

BOATING: Allowed in 40-acre Newton Lake. Car-top boat access and ramp.

FISHING: Permitted in the lake, with fishing piers.

WINTER ACTIVITIES: Cross-country skiing.

> **For additional information:**
> Camden County Department of Parks
> 1301 Park Boulevard
> Cherry Hill, NJ 08002–3752
> Telephone: (856) 216-2117

Parvin State Park

Almond Road • 1,309 acres

LOCATION: From Route 55 north or south, take exit 35. Follow signs to the park. The park is located between Centerton and Vineland, on Route 540.

HOURS: The grounds are open from dawn to dusk. The park office is open daily, Memorial Day weekend through Labor Day, from 8:30 A.M. to 6:00 P.M., and on Friday until 8:00 P.M. Off-season hours are daily, from 8:30 A.M. to 4:00 P.M.

ENTRANCE FEE: Fee charged for use of the beach area.

HANDICAP ACCESS: Two cabins are handicap accessible. In the camping area, toilets and showers are accessible. One of the trails is wheelchair accessible. The bathhouse is handicap accessible.

DESCRIPTION: The park is named after the Parvin family, who owned and operated a grist- and sawmill on Parvin Pond. The park offers a full range of activities.

CABINS: Fifteen cabins, each with a furnished living room, with a fireplace or wood-burning stove; two rooms with double-deck bunks; a kitchen with running water, an electric stove, and a refrigerator; and a bathroom with a sink, a toilet, and a shower. There is electricity. The living room can be opened to a screened porch. A brick patio has a table and grill. Each cabin accommodates four people. Two additional cabins have recently been constructed and are accessible for people with disabilities. Cabins are on the north shore of Thundergust Lake. Open April 1 through October 31.

CAMPING: Fifty-six sites for tents and trailers along the south shore of Parvin Lake are open from March 1 through November 30. Modern restrooms with hot showers, laundry, and a dumping station are provided. A boat launch and bathing area are available for campers.

PICNICKING: Tables, with grills, with a playground and a restroom in the beach area.

BOATING: Trailer and car-top boat launch on Parvin Lake. Electric motors only. Canoes can be rented at the concession stand. For more information, call (609) 358-3240. Canoes can be launched at Thundergust Lake; there is no ramp.

FISHING: Permitted in 95-acre Parvin Lake, 14-acre Thundergust Lake, and in streams in the park.

SWIMMING: At Parvin Lake, a lifeguard-supervised sand beach has a bathhouse, restrooms, and a food concession. The beach is open from Memorial Day weekend through Labor Day.

HIKING: Fifteen miles of trails and sand roads.

MOUNTAIN BIKING: Permitted on trails.

HORSEBACK RIDING: Permitted on some trails.

For additional information:
701 Almond Road
Pittsgrove, NJ 08318–3928
Telephone: (856) 358-8616

 # Pemberton Lake
Wildlife Management Area

Burlington County   ◆   82 acres

LOCATION: Located north of Route 70, and south of the town of Pemberton.

HOURS: Dawn to dusk.

ENTRANCE FEE: None.

HANDICAP ACCESS: None.

BOATING: Car-top access to 20-acre Pemberton Lake.

FISHING: Permitted in the lake.

> **For additional information:**
> New Jersey Division of Fish and Wildlife
> Trenton Office
> 501 E. State Street, P.O. Box 400
> Trenton, NJ 08625–0400
> Telephone: (609) 984-0547

Penn State Forest

Burlington County ♦ 3,366 acres

LOCATION: Located east of Wharton State Forest, near the town of Speedwell.

HOURS: Dawn to dusk.

ENTRANCE FEE: None.

HANDICAP ACCESS: None.

SPECIAL FEATURES
> **Pine Barren Plains**—Rare occurrence of pine and oak forests with trees that attain a height of only about four feet at maturity.

BOATING: Allowed in 92-acre Lake Oswego, with car-top boat launch.

FISHING: Permitted in the lake.

HIKING: Miles of sand roads.

MOUNTAIN BIKING: Permitted on sand roads.

HORSEBACK RIDING: Permitted on sand roads.

HUNTING: Permitted in designated areas (3,360 acres), for deer, small game, turkey, and waterfowl.

WINTER ACTIVITIES: Cross-country skiing.

> **For additional information:**
> c/o Bass River State Forest
> P.O. Box 118
> New Gretna, NJ 08224
> Telephone: (609) 296-1114

Frog.

Rancocas State Park

Hainesport and Westampton Townships ◆ *Burlington County* ◆ *1,252 acres*

LOCATION: Located east of I–295, exits 43 and 45, and north of Route 537.

HOURS: The grounds are open from dawn to dusk. The New Jersey Audubon Nature Center is open Tuesday through Saturday, from 9:00 A.M. to 5:00 P.M., and Sunday, from 12:00 P.M. to 5:00 P.M.

ENTRANCE FEE: None.

HANDICAP ACCESS: The Nature Center is handicap accessible.

SPECIAL FEATURES

New Jersey Audubon Nature Center—Exhibits, small animal displays, restrooms, library, and information. For more information, call (609) 261-2595.

FISHING: Permitted in the Rancocas Creek, for pickerel and catfish.

HIKING: Marked and unmarked trails, in addition to a self-guided nature trail at the Nature Center.

HUNTING: Permitted in designated areas (626 acres), for deer; bow-hunting only.

For additional information:
c/o Brendan T. Byrne State Forest
P.O. Box 215
New Lisbon, NJ 08064
Telephone: (609) 726-1191; or

New Jersey Audubon Nature Center
794 Rancocas Road
Mount Holly, NJ 08060

Red Bank Battlefield Park

100 Hessian Avenue ◆ National Park, Gloucester County ◆
44 acres

LOCATION: Located west of the town of National Park. Access is from Route 130 and I–295.

HOURS: Dawn to dusk.

ENTRANCE FEE: None.

HANDICAP ACCESS: The fishing pier and picnic area are handicap accessible.

SPECIAL FEATURES
James and Ann Whitall House (1748)—Served as a hospital after the Battle of Red Bank.

PICNICKING: Tables with grills, with a playground and a restroom.

FISHING: Permitted in the Delaware River.

For additional information:
Gloucester County Parks & Recreation
6 Blackwell-Barnsboro Road
Sewell, NJ 08081
Telephone: (609) 468-0100; Fax: (609) 468-4497

Salem River Wildlife Management Area

Salem County ◆ 2,430 acres

LOCATION: Southeast of exit 1 of the New Jersey Turnpike.

HOURS: Dawn to dusk.

ENTRANCE FEE: None.

HANDICAP ACCESS: Observation tower located near Route 45.

BOATING: Car-top boat launch at Game Creek, which leads into Salem River.

FISHING: In Salem River.

HIKING: Informal trails in the tract located near Route 45.

HUNTING: Deer, small game, turkey, and waterfowl.

> **For additional information:**
> New Jersey Division of Fish and Wildlife
> Trenton Office
> 501 E. State Street, P.O. Box 400
> Trenton, NJ 08625–0400
> Telephone: (609) 984-0547

 # Scotland Run Park

*Academy Street • Franklinville, Gloucester County •
940 acres*

LOCATION: Located east of Route 47, and south of Route 536, at the intersection of Route 655 (Fries Mill Road) and Route 610 (Clayton-Williamstown Road).

HOURS: The grounds are open from dawn to dusk. The Nature Center is open, Tuesday through Thursday, from 8:30 A.M. to 1:00 P.M., and by appointment.

ENTRANCE FEE: None.

HANDICAP ACCESS: The Nature Center, fishing and boating area, picnic area, playground, restrooms, and nature trail are handicap accessible.

SPECIAL FEATURES

Scotland Run Park Nature Center—Displays of flora and fauna of the area. Restrooms are available. For more information, call (856) 881-0845.

PICNICKING: Tables with grills, a playground, and restrooms.

BOATING: Allowed in eighty-acre Wilson Lake. A boat launch is available for car-top and trailer boats.

FISHING: Permitted in the lake.

HIKING: Two self-guided nature trails. A map is available.

For additional information:
Gloucester County Parks & Recreation
6 Blackwell-Barnsboro Road
Sewell, NJ 08081
Telephone: (609) 468-0100; Fax: (609) 468-4497

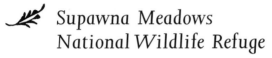 Supawna Meadows National Wildlife Refuge

Pennsville Township, Salem County ◆ 2,874 *acres*

LOCATION: Located west of Route 49, adjacent to the southeastern portion of Fort Mott State Park.

HOURS: Dawn to dusk.

ENTRANCE FEE: None.

HANDICAP ACCESS: None.

SPECIAL FEATURES
> **Finns Point Rear Range Light**—Listed in the National Register of Historic Places. Open to the public on the third Sunday of the month, April through October, from 12:00 P.M. to 4:00 P.M.

FISHING: Permitted in the Salem River, in designated areas.

CRABBING: Permitted in the Salem River, in designated areas.

HIKING: Marked trails.

HUNTING: For deer and waterfowl, with a permit.

For additional information:
197 Lighthouse Road
Pennsville, NJ 08070
Telephone: (856) 935-1487; Fax: (856) 935-1198

Swan Bay Wildlife Management Area

Burlington County ◆ 1,875 *acres*

LOCATION: Located south of Route 542, and west of the Garden State Parkway, exit 50. Access is from Turtle Creek Road.

HOURS: Dawn to dusk.

ENTRANCE FEE: None.

HANDICAP ACCESS: None.

BOATING: Car-top access.

FISHING: Permitted in the Mullica River, Wading River, and Turtle Creek, off Route 542.

HUNTING: For deer, small game, and waterfowl.

For additional information:
New Jersey Division of Fish and Wildlife
Trenton Office
501 E. State Street, P.O. Box 400
Trenton, NJ 08625–0400
Telephone: (609) 984-0547

 # Thundergust Pond
Wildlife Management Area

Salem County • 1,249 acres

LOCATION: Located east of Route 49, and west of the town of Friesburg.

HOURS: Dawn to dusk.

ENTRANCE FEE: None.

HANDICAP ACCESS: None.

BOATING: Car-top boat access to 14-acre lake.

FISHING: Permitted in the lake.

HIKING: Informal trails.

MOUNTAIN BIKING: Allowed on existing trails and secondary roads on wildlife management areas from March 1 to April 15, and from June 1 to September 15, as well as on all Sundays throughout the year.

HORSEBACK RIDING: Allowed on all trails, with a permit.

HUNTING: For deer, small game, turkey, and waterfowl.

WINTER ACTIVITIES: Cross-country skiing can be enjoyed on all of the trails in the tract on Sunday.

For additional information:
New Jersey Division of Fish and Wildlife
Trenton Office
501 E. State Street, P.O. Box 400
Trenton, NJ 08625–0400
Telephone: (609) 984-0547

Wharton State Forest

Atlantic, Burlington, and Camden Counties • *114,557 acres*

LOCATION: The Atsion Ranger Station is located at the intersection of Route 206, Quackerbridge Road, and Atsion Road in Atsion. Batsto Village is located on Route 542, 13 miles east of Hammonton.

HOURS: The grounds are open from dawn to dusk. The Nature Center is open daily, Memorial Day weekend through Labor Day, from 10:00 A.M. to 4:00 P.M.; during the spring and fall, Wednesday through Sunday, from 10:00 A.M. to 4:00 P.M.; and during the winter (December–March), Tuesday through Saturday, from 12:30 P.M. to 4:00 P.M.

The Atsion Ranger Station is open daily, Memorial Day weekend to Labor Day, from 9:00 A.M. to 4:00 P.M.; Friday and Saturday until 9:00 P.M. Call for hours during the rest of the year.

The Atsion Recreation Area is open daily, Memorial Day weekend to Labor Day, from 9:00 A.M. to 8:00 P.M.; swimming can be enjoyed from 10:00 A.M. to 6:00 P.M. The recreation area is open (except for swimming) in September, from 9:00 A.M. to 6:00 P.M. Call for other hours.

Batsto Village is open daily, from 9:00 A.M. to 4:00 P.M.; Batsto Visitor Center is open daily, from 9:00 A.M. to 4:30 P.M.

ENTRANCE FEE: A fee is charged for the Atsion Recreation Area, from Memorial Day weekend through Labor Day. A fee is also charged for Batsto Village during the summer, on weekends and holidays.

HANDICAP ACCESS: The nature trail at the Nature Center is wheelchair accessible, and most of the cabins are accessible, as are Atsion and Batsto ranger stations, and Batsto Nature Center.

DESCRIPTION: Located in the heart of the Pine Barrens, Wharton is the largest park in the state system. The area experienced its greatest growth around the time of the Revolutionary War, with the exploitation of the bog ore found along the area streams and in the area swamps. By the mid-nineteenth century, with iron-ore discoveries in Pennsylvania and West Virginia, the area was in decline. From 1876 to 1906, Joseph Wharton, a Philadelphia industrialist, acquired most of the land encompassing the present-day tract. The state acquired the land in 1954 and 1955.

Batsto, Wharton State Forest.

(photo credit: Greg Johnson)

SPECIAL FEATURES

Batsto Nature Center—Displays and exhibits of flora and fauna, small live animals, and restrooms nearby. For more information, call (609) 567-4559.

Batona Trail—Begun in 1961, the Batona Trail today spans approximately fifty miles, starting in Brendan Byrne State Forest, and continuing through the Wharton and Bass River state forests. It is maintained jointly by the Batona Hiking Club and the Park Service. The trail can be reached by car at many points, enabling hikes of varying lengths. A map of the trail is available at park offices.

Batsto Village—Founded in 1766, the village consists of thirty-three historic buildings and structures, including the Batsto Mansion, gristmill, sawmill, general store, workers' homes, and post office. For more information, call (609) 561-3262.

CABINS: Eight cabins, situated along the north shore of Atsion Lake, near the Atsion Ranger Station, are available for weekly rental from April 1 to October 31. Cabins 4 and 8 sleep eight, and the rest sleep four. All have indoor toilets and showers with hot and cold water, bunk beds, rustic furnishings, and a full kitchen. Eating and

Wharton State Forest.

cooking utensils and bedding are not provided. Cabins 6 through 9 are set further back from the road, for those concerned about small children being near cars. Each cabin also has tables and a grill outside, and they are situated so that there is adequate privacy.

CAMPING: Fifty tent and trailer sites, with fire rings and picnic tables. Potable water, flush toilets, and showers are within walking distance. Ground fires are not permitted during the day. A trailer sanitary station is open from March 1 through November 30. Campsites are open from April 1 through December 31. There are also a number of other camping areas near the Batona Trail, or alongside one of the rivers in the park.

PICNICKING: Tables with grills, at Crowley Landing and at Atsion day-use complex. The Atsion picnic area, near the bathing beach, also has a playground and restrooms.

BOATING: Four rivers flow through the forest, providing excellent canoeing opportunities. The Mullica, the Batsto, the West Branch of the Wading, and the Oswego River all have major canoe trails. A public boat launch for motorized boats is located at Crowley Landing on the Mullica River. The lakes in the forest are restricted to electric motors under 5 horsepower.

FISHING: Permitted in all of the waterways within the forest.

SWIMMING: A lifeguard-supervised sand beach is located at the Atsion Recreation Area. There are restrooms, changing rooms, a food concession, and first aid.

HIKING: Close to 500 miles of sand roads and 75 miles of mostly unmarked trails. Nature trails have also been established in the Batsto Natural Area, and self-guiding trail brochures are available at the Nature Center.

MOUNTAIN BIKING: Permitted on close to 500 miles of unimproved sand and dirt roads.

HORSEBACK RIDING: Permitted on close to 500 miles of unimproved sand and dirt roads.

HUNTING: Permitted in designated areas (108,671 acres), for deer, small game, turkey, and waterfowl.

WINTER ACTIVITIES: Cross-country skiing.

For additional information:

Batsto Visitor Center
4110 Nesco Road
Hammonton, NJ 08037
Telephone: (609) 561-0024; or

Atsion Office
744 Route 206
Shamong, NJ 08088
Telephone: (609) 268-0444

White Oak Branch Wildlife Management Area

Gloucester County ◆ *1,305 acres*

LOCATION: Located west of Route 322, and north of the town of Downstown.

HOURS: Dawn to dusk.

ENTRANCE FEE: None.

HANDICAP ACCESS: None.

HIKING: Informal trails and sand roads.

MOUNTAIN BIKING: Allowed on existing trails and secondary roads on wildlife management areas from March 1 to April 15, and from June 1 to September 15, as well as on all Sundays throughout the year.

HORSEBACK RIDING: Allowed on all trails, with a permit.

HUNTING: For deer, small game, turkey, and waterfowl.

WINTER ACTIVITIES: Cross-country skiing can be enjoyed on all of the trails in the tract on Sunday.

For additional information:
New Jersey Division of Fish and Wildlife
Trenton Office
501 E. State Street, P.O. Box 400
Trenton, NJ 08625–0400
Telephone: (609) 984-0547

Winslow Wildlife Management Area

Camden and Gloucester Counties ◆ *7,338 acres*

LOCATION: Located west of the Atlantic City Expressway, exit 33W.

HOURS: Dawn to dusk.

ENTRANCE FEE: None.

HANDICAP ACCESS: None.

BOATING: Allowed in 12-acre Oak Pond, with boat ramp and car-top access.

FISHING: Permitted in the lake.

HIKING: Informal trails and sand roads.

MOUNTAIN BIKING: Allowed on existing trails and secondary roads on wildlife management areas from March 1 to April 15, and from June 1 to September 15, as well as on all Sundays throughout the year.

HORSEBACK RIDING: Allowed on all trails, with a permit.

HUNTING: For deer, small game, turkey, and waterfowl.

WINTER ACTIVITIES: Cross-country skiing can be enjoyed on all of the trails in the tract on Sunday.

For additional information:
New Jersey Division of Fish and Wildlife
Trenton Office
501 E. State Street, P.O. Box 400
Trenton, NJ 08625—0400
Telephone: (609) 984-0547

Region Six

Atlantic, Cape May,
& Cumberland Counties

Allan I. Marcus

Belleplain State Forest.

ATLANTIC

CUMBERLAND

206
24
23
37
16
563
GSP
9
1
322
28
54
42
ATLANTIC CITY
27
MAYS LANDING
20
4
43
36
18
38
29
39
40
35
21
5
49
30
31
50
12
6
55
22
32
GARDEN STATE PRWY.
13
553
11
555
10
15
DIVIDING
CREEK
3
34
33
47
19
17
25
14
2
7
CAPE
MAY
41
9

- N -

Parks
Selected Towns
Selected Roads
County Borders

0   5
miles

8

26
9
CAPE MAY

1 Absecon Wildlife Management Area
2 Beaver Swamp Wildlife Management Area
3 Belleplain State Forest
4 Birch Grove Park
5 Bridgeton City Park
6 Buckshutem Wildlife Management Area
7 Cape May County Park
8 Cape May National Wildlife Refuge
9 Cape May Point State Park
10 Cape May Wetlands Wildlife Management Area
11 Cedarville Ponds Wildlife Management Area
12 Clarks Pond Wildlife Management Area
13 Corson's Inlet State Park
14 Dennis Creek Wildlife Management Area
15 Dix Wildlife Management Area
16 Edwin B. Forsythe National Wildlife Refuge—Brigantine Division
17 Egg Island Wildlife Management Area
18 Estell Manor Park
19 Fortescue Wildlife Management Area
20 Gaskill Park
21 Gibson Creek Wildlife Management Area
22 Gum Tree Corner Wildlife Management Area
23 Hammonton Creek Wildlife Management Area
24 Hammonton Lake Park
25 Heislerville Wildlife Management Area
26 Higbee Beach Wildlife Management Area
27 Lenape Park
28 Makepeace Lake Wildlife Management Area
29 Maple Lake Wildlife Management Area
30 Maurice River Wildlife Management Area
31 Menantico Ponds Wildlife Management Area
32 Millville Wildlife Management Area
33 Nantuxent Wildlife Management Area
34 New Sweden Wildlife Management Area
35 Peaslee Wildlife Management Area
36 Pork Island Wildlife Management Area
37 Port Republic Wildlife Management Area
38 River Bend
39 Tuckahoe Wildlife Management Area
40 Union Lake Wildlife Management Area
41 The Wetlands Institute
42 Weymouth County Park
43 Whirlpool Island County Park

Absecon Wildlife Management Area

Route 87, Atlantic County • 3,756 acres

LOCATION: Located north of Route 87 and Atlantic City, in Absecon and Reeds Bay. Adjacent to Brigantine National Wildlife Refuge.

HOURS: Dawn to dusk.

ENTRANCE FEE: None.

HANDICAP ACCESS: None.

BOATING: Allowed in the bay. Boat ramp is available.

FISHING: Saltwater fishing in coastal bays and creeks.

CRABBING: Permitted in coastal bays and creeks.

HUNTING: For waterfowl.

For additional information:
New Jersey Division of Fish and Wildlife
Trenton Office
501 E. State Street, P.O. Box 400
Trenton, NJ 08625–0400
Telephone: (609) 984-0547

 ## Beaver Swamp Wildlife Management Area

Beaver Dam Road • Swainton, Cape May County • 2,907 acres

LOCATION: Located east of Route 585 (Court House–South Dennis Road) and south of Route 83.

HOURS: Dawn to dusk.

ENTRANCE FEE: None.

HANDICAP ACCESS: None.

FISHING: Fishing is fair, for white perch and pickerel.

CRABBING: Permitted in waterways.

MOUNTAIN BIKING: Allowed on existing trails and secondary roads from March 1 to April 15, and from June 1 to September 15, as well as on all Sundays throughout the year.

HUNTING: For deer, small game, wild turkey, and waterfowl.

WINTER ACTIVITIES: Cross-country skiing on all trails on Sunday.

For additional information:
New Jersey Division of Fish and Wildlife
Trenton Office
501 E. State Street, P.O. Box 400
Trenton, NJ 08625–0400
Telephone: (609) 984-0547

 ## Belleplain State Forest

Meisle Road, Woodbine ◆ Cape May and Cumberland
Counties ◆ 20,749 acres

LOCATION: From Route 550, about 1.5 miles west of Woodbine, turn southwest onto Henkin-Sifkin Road. Take the next turn into the park.

HOURS: The grounds are open from dawn to dusk. The park office is open daily, Memorial Day weekend through Labor Day, from 9:00 A.M. to 11:00 P.M.; and off-season, daily, from 8:30 A.M. to 4:00 P.M. Call for Friday and Saturday evening hours. The Interpretive Center is open daily, Memorial Day weekend through Labor Day, from 8:30 A.M. to 4:00 P.M.; off-season, it is open on weekends only.

ENTRANCE FEE: Fee charged from Memorial Day weekend through Labor Day.

Sundew plant at Bennett Boggs, Belleplain.

HANDICAP ACCESS: Yurts and lean-tos are handicap accessible, as are the beach area, the picnic area, and restrooms.

DESCRIPTION: Centered around 26-acre Lake Nummy, a former cranberry bog and reservoir, the state forest offers extensive camping opportunities and related activities.

SPECIAL FEATURES

Interpretive Center—Displays and exhibits of area flora and fauna. For more information, call (609) 861-1354.

YURTS: There are five yurts: circular tents built on a wood frame, featuring wood floors, a deck, and a Plexiglas skylight. Each yurt has a lockable wood door, window screens and flaps, and two double-deck bunks, which sleep up to four people. Accessible to people with disabilities.

LEAN-TOS: Fourteen fully enclosed lean-tos are available in the Meisle Field area for year-round camping. Each consists of one unfurnished room, accommodating up to six people. Each site has a picnic table, fire ring, metal grill, and wood-burning stove for heat. Showers and laundry facilities are within walking distance.

CAMPING: There are three family camping areas—at least one is open all year—with a total of 169 sites. Each site has a picnic table and fire ring. Parking spaces at most sites will accommodate a trailer. One dumping station for trailers is available at the CCC camping area from March 1 through November 30. No individual water, electric, or sewer connections are available. Flush toilets, hot showers, and a laundry are maintained in each camping area. The CCC and North Shore campgrounds have a playground.

PICNICKING: In shaded area near the beach. Tables and grills, with a playground and a restroom nearby.

BOATING: Small boats and canoes may be launched at specific locations on 26-acre Lake Nummy, as well as on East Creek Pond. Gas motors are not permitted. A canoe concession is operated during the summer months on Lake Nummy, near the bathing beach. For more information, call (609) 861-2980.

FISHING: Permitted in Lake Nummy and in East Creek Pond. Pickerel, perch, and catfish are the primary species.

SWIMMING: A lifeguard-supervised beach is located on the north side of Lake Nummy. It includes parking, a bathhouse, playground equipment, and a refreshment concession that is open during the peak summer months.

HIKING: A 6.5-mile hiking trail connects Lake Nummy and East Creek Pond. In addition, there are many miles of unimproved roads suitable for year-round hiking. A self-guided nature trail is located near the eastern end of Lake Nummy.

MOUNTAIN BIKING: Permitted on some trails.

HORSEBACK RIDING: Permitted on some trails.

HUNTING: Permitted in designated areas (18,223 acres), for deer, small game, turkey, and waterfowl.

WINTER ACTIVITIES: Cross-country skiing.

For additional information:
P.O. Box 450
Woodbine, NJ 08270
Telephone: (609) 861-2404

 # Birch Grove Park

Burton Avenue • Northfield, Atlantic County •
271 acres

LOCATION: Located east of the Garden State Parkway, exit 36. The park is two blocks from the intersection of Route 9 (New Road) and Mill Road, on Burton Avenue.

HOURS: The grounds are open from 7:00 A.M. to 7:00 P.M.; the Nature Center and park office are open daily, from 9:00 A.M. to 5:00 P.M.

ENTRANCE FEE: There is a fee charged to out-of-town visitors on weekends.

HANDICAP ACCESS: Boardwalks and ramps give access to some of the lakes for fishing. A picnic area and restrooms are also handicap accessible.

CAMPING: Fifty-one sites for tents and trailers, with a restroom, showers, and drinking water. Electric, sewage, and water hookups are available. A refreshment concession operates during the summer. Camping is available from the first Saturday in April through Columbus Day in October.

PICNICKING: Tables, with a playground and a restroom.

FISHING: Permitted in the many lakes, which are stocked with trout. Also present are chain pickerel, largemouth bass, and pan fish.

HIKING: Seven marked trails.

> **For additional information:**
> Burton Avenue
> Northfield, NJ 08225
> Telephone: (609) 641-3778

 # Bridgeton City Park

Park Drive ◆ *Bridgeton, Cumberland County* ◆ *1,100 acres*

LOCATION: Take Route 49 to West Drive, and head north to Park Drive. Turn east on Park Drive for the beach and the zoo.

HOURS: The grounds are open from dawn to dusk; the park office is open, Monday through Friday, from 8:30 A.M. to 4:00 P.M. The zoo is open during the spring and summer, from 10:00 A.M. to 6:00 P.M., and during the fall and winter, from 9:00 A.M. to 4:00 P.M. The Nail Mill Museum is open, Tuesday through Friday, from 10:30 A.M. to 3:30 P.M., and on weekends, from 11:00 A.M. to 4:00 P.M.

ENTRANCE FEE: None.

HANDICAP ACCESS: The zoo, a picnic area, fishing, and a playground are handicap accessible.

SPECIAL FEATURES

Cohanzick Zoo—The first zoo in New Jersey, established in 1934. It has more than two hundred birds and mammals from around the world. Admission is free. For more information, call (856) 455-3230.

Nail Mill Museum—Displays of early iron tools, glass, and local history. For more information, call (856) 455-4100.

New Sweden Farmstead Museum—Seventeenth-century Swedish settler's farmstead. For more information, call (856) 455-9785.

BOATING: Allowed in 88-acre Sunset Lake, and in 18-acre Mary Elmer Lake. Both lakes have trailer and car-top boat launches. Bridgeton Canoe & Kayak supplies boats to Sunset Lake, from May through September. For more information, call (856) 453-0887.

SWIMMING: Lifeguard-supervised swimming can be enjoyed at Sunset Lake, from Memorial Day weekend through Labor Day.

FISHING: Permitted in both lakes.

HIKING: Several marked trails.

PICNICKING: At various locations throughout the park, with tables, grills, playgrounds, and restrooms.

For additional information:
City Hall Annex
181 E. Commerce Street
Bridgeton, NJ 08302

Buckshutem
Wildlife Management Area

Cumberland County ◆ 3,136 acres

LOCATION: Located south of Route 49, near Gouldtown.

HOURS: Dawn to dusk.

ENTRANCE FEE: None.

HANDICAP ACCESS: None.

HIKING: Informal trails.

MOUNTAIN BIKING: Allowed on existing trails and secondary roads from March 1 to April 15, and from June 1 to September 15, as well as on all Sundays throughout the year.

HUNTING: For deer, small game, and turkey.

WINTER ACTIVITIES: Cross-country skiing on all trails on Sunday.

For additional information:
New Jersey Division of Fish and Wildlife
Trenton Office
501 E. State Street, P.O. Box 400
Trenton, NJ 08625–0400
Telephone: (609) 984-0547

Cape May County Park

Route 9 and Pine Lane ◆ Cape May Court House,
Cape May County ◆ 128 acres

LOCATION: Take the Garden State Parkway to exit 11, and travel west. This road leads directly to the park.

HOURS: The grounds are open during the summer, from 9:00 A.M. to dusk; and during the winter, from 9:00 A.M. to 5:00 P.M. The zoo is open daily, from 10:00 A.M. to 4:45 P.M.

ENTRANCE FEE: None.

HANDICAP ACCESS: Wheelchairs are available at the park and at the zoo.

SPECIAL FEATURES

Zoo—Very well-maintained zoo, with more than 180 different species of animals. For more information, call (609) 465-5271.

FISHING: Permitted in pond.

HIKING: Marked hiking and nature trails.

PICNICKING: Picnic areas are scattered all over the park, with playgrounds and restrooms convenient to most of the sites.

For additional information:
4 Moore Road, DN 801
Cape May Courthouse, NJ 08210

 Cape May National Wildlife Refuge

Cape May County ◆ 8,000 acres

LOCATION: From the Garden State Parkway, turn west at exit 10. Go into Cape May Court House. At Route 9, turn left (south). Go through the next light, and make a right at Hand Avenue. Continue to State Highway 47. Turn left (south) onto Route 47, then make a quick right (west) onto Kimbles Beach Road. The refuge office is about one-eighth of a mile on the right.

HOURS: The grounds are open from dawn to dusk; the refuge office is open weekdays, from 8:00 A.M. to 4:00 P.M.

ENTRANCE FEE: None.

HANDICAP ACCESS: See information for individual units.

Delaware Bay Division

10,000+ acres

LOCATION: In Middle Township, along the Delaware Bay.

HOURS: Dawn to dusk.

ENTRANCE FEE: None.

HANDICAP ACCESS: The park office and both marked trails are handicap accessible.

FISHING: There is surf fishing.

HIKING: Two marked trails.

HUNTING: Permitted in designated areas, for deer and waterfowl.

Great Cedar Swamp Division

10,000+ acres

LOCATION: Straddles Dennis and Upper Townships.

HOURS: Dawn to dusk.

ENTRANCE FEE: None.

HANDICAP ACCESS: None.

HIKING: Informal trails.

HUNTING: Permitted in designated areas, for deer and waterfowl.

Two Mile Beach Unit

500+ acres

LOCATION: In Lower Township, just south of Wildwood Crest.

HOURS: Dawn to dusk.

ENTRANCE FEE: None.

HANDICAP ACCESS: The boardwalk trail is handicap accessible, and a viewing platform is accessible.

FISHING: Surf fishing.

HIKING: Marked trail, with wildlife viewing platform.

HUNTING: Permitted in designated areas for deer and waterfowl.

For additional information:

Cape May National Wildlife Refuge
24 Kimbles Beach Road
Cape May Court House, NJ 08210–2078
Telephone: (609) 463-0994

Cape May Point State Park

Lighthouse Avenue • Cape May Point, Cape May County •
235 acres

LOCATION: Located south of Sunset Boulevard, in Cape May Point.

HOURS: The grounds are open from dawn to dusk. The park office is open, Memorial Day weekend to Labor Day, from 8:00 A.M. to 8:00 P.M.; open off-season, daily, from 8:00 A.M. to 4:30 P.M. For more information, call (609) 884-2159.

ENTRANCE FEE: None.

HANDICAP ACCESS: There is access to the nature area, restrooms, the nature trail, and the approach/overlook to the beach.

DESCRIPTION: Formerly used as a coastal defense base and a radio transmitter station, this park was established in 1974, and is today one of the more popular sites for birdwatching in North America. Due to its location (a merging point for a number of northern and southern species of vegetation) and diversity of habitats, the park supports a great variety of wildlife and plants.

Courtesy of Cape May Point State Park

Cape May Point State Park.

The lighthouse—Built in 1859, the 157-foot-high lighthouse is open to visitors daily, Memorial Day through Labor Day, from 9:00 A.M. to 8:00 P.M. For more information, call (609) 884-5404.

Nature Center/Museum—Exhibits of the natural and cultural history of the area.

FISHING: Surf fishing.

HIKING: More than three miles of trails and boardwalks, including a one-half mile trail accessible to the handicapped.

PICNICKING: Three sheltered areas, with tables and grills.

BIRDWATCHING: The tip of Cape May is one of the most popular sites in North America for viewing the fall bird migration. A hawk-watch platform has also been erected, with views of the marsh.

For additional information:
P.O. Box 107
Cape May Point, NJ 08212

Cape May Wetlands Wildlife Management Area

Cape May County • 12,423 acres

LOCATION: Located east of the Garden State Parkway, exit 10, near the town of Stone Harbor.

HOURS: Dawn to dusk.

ENTRANCE FEE: None.

HANDICAP ACCESS: None.

BOATING: Allowed in the bay.

FISHING: Permitted in the bay and in the creeks.

CRABBING: Permitted in the bay and in the creeks.

HUNTING: For waterfowl.

For additional information:
New Jersey Division of Fish and Wildlife
Trenton Office
501 E. State Street, P.O. Box 400
Trenton, NJ 08625–0400
Telephone: (609) 984-0547

✒ Cedarville Ponds
Wildlife Management Area

Sawmill Road and Route 533, Cumberland County ◆ 42 acres

LOCATION: Located east of the intersection of Sawmill Road and Route 553, in Cedarville. Access is from Sawmill Road (south of the railroad tracks), and also from Route 553, about 0.5 miles south of its intersection with Sawmill Road.

HOURS: Dawn to dusk.

ENTRANCE FEE: None.

HANDICAP ACCESS: None.

FISHING: Restricted to shore fishing. Species present include largemouth bass, chain pickerel, bluegill, and brown bullhead.

> **For additional information:**
> *New Jersey Division of Fish and Wildlife*
> Trenton Office
> 501 E. State Street, P.O. Box 400
> Trenton, NJ 08625—0400
> Telephone: (609) 984-0547

✒ Clarks Pond Wildlife Management Area

Route 698 (Millville Road), Cumberland County ◆ 201 acres

LOCATION: Located south of route 553 (Fairton-Gouldtown Road), west of Route 638 (Burlington Road), and northeast of Fairton.

HOURS: Dawn to dusk.

ENTRANCE FEE: None.

HANDICAP ACCESS: None.

BOATING: Car-top boats and electric motors are permitted on all three ponds.

FISHING: Fishing is fair to good in all three ponds, for a variety of fish.

> **For additional information:**
> *New Jersey Division of Fish and Wildlife*
> Trenton Office
> 501 E. State Street, P.O. Box 400
> Trenton, NJ 08625—0400
> Telephone: (609) 984-0547

Cedarville Ponds Wildlife Management Area.

Roger R. Locandro

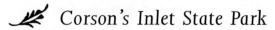

Corson's Inlet State Park

Cape May County ◆ *341 acres*

LOCATION: Located East of the Garden State Parkway, exit 25. The park is bisected by Ocean Drive (Route 619).

HOURS: Dawn to dusk.

ENTRANCE FEE: Fee charged for boat launch, Memorial Day weekend through Labor Day.

HANDICAP ACCESS: None.

BOATING: Boat ramp for trailer and car-top.

FISHING: Saltwater fishing, especially at Rush-Chatten Bridge.

CRABBING: Permitted.

HIKING: Three marked trails, ranging from 0.5 miles to 1.5 miles.

> **For additional information:**
> *c/o Belleplain State Forest*
> *P.O. Box 450*
> *Woodbine, NJ 08270*
> *Telephone: (609) 861-2404*

Dennis Creek Wildlife Management Area

Route 47, Cape May County ◆ *6,147 acres*

LOCATION: Located west and south of Route 47, on the Delaware Bay, northwest of Goshen.

HOURS: Dawn to dusk.

ENTRANCE FEE: None.

HANDICAP ACCESS: None.

DESCRIPTION: One of the finest state-owned salt marshes, known for its abundance and diversity of animal life.

BOATING: A boat ramp is located at the main parking area, by Dennis Creek, as well as at Jakes Landing Road and Bidwells Ditch.

FISHING: The tidal creeks offer excellent fishing for white perch and striped bass.

CRABBING: Permitted in the tidal creeks.

HUNTING: For small game and waterfowl.

For additional information:
New Jersey Division of Fish and Wildlife
Trenton Office
501 E. State Street, P.O. Box 400
Trenton, NJ 08625–0400
Telephone: (609) 984-0547

Dix Wildlife Management Area

Back Neck Road • Fairfield Township, Cumberland
County • 2,643 acres

LOCATION: Six miles west of Fairton, on the Delaware Bay.

HOURS: Dawn to dusk.

ENTRANCE FEE: None.

HANDICAP ACCESS: None.

FISHING: Good saltwater fishing in the streams and creeks.

CRABBING: Permitted in the streams and creeks.

HUNTING: For deer, small game, turkey, and waterfowl.

Note: This area supports New Jersey's last well-established, nesting bald-eagle pair. It is also an important feeding area for wintering bald eagles.

For additional information:
New Jersey Division of Fish and Wildlife
Trenton Office
501 E. State Street, P.O. Box 400
Trenton, NJ 08625–0400
Telephone: (609) 984-0547

Edwin B. Forsythe National Wildlife Refuge—Brigantine Division

Great Creek Road • Oceanville, Atlantic County • 24,000 acres

LOCATION: Located east of Route 9, and north of Route 30, in the vicinity of Oceanville.

HOURS: The grounds are open from dawn to dusk; the office is open weekdays, from 8:00 A.M. to 4:00 P.M.

ENTRANCE FEE: Fee year-round.

HANDICAP ACCESS: None.

FISHING: Permitted in designated areas.

CRABBING: Permitted in designated areas.

HIKING: Two short, loop nature trails of less than 0.5 miles each wind through upland forest and marsh.

HUNTING: Permitted in designated areas, for deer and waterfowl.

> **For additional information:**
> Great Creek Road
> P.O. Box 72
> Oceanville, NJ 08231
> Telephone: (609) 652-1474

Egg Island Wildlife Management Area

Cumberland County ♦ *8,832 acres*

LOCATION: The tract is located east of Fortescue, and south of Route 553.

HOURS: Dawn to dusk.

ENTRANCE FEE: None.

FISHING: Excellent fishing for white perch in the tidal creeks. Weakfish, bluefish, fluke, and sea bass can be caught in Delaware Bay.

CRABBING: Permitted in Delaware Bay.

BIRDWATCHING: Peregrine falcon nesting towers.

HUNTING: For small game and waterfowl.

> **For additional information:**
> New Jersey Division of Fish and Wildlife
> Trenton Office
> 501 E. State Street, P.O. Box 400
> Trenton, NJ 08625–0400
> Telephone: (609) 984-0547

Estell Manor Park

Route 50 ♦ *Estellville, Atlantic County* ♦ *1,672 acres*

LOCATION: Off the east side of Route 50, 3 miles south of Mays Landing.

HOURS: The grounds are open from 7:30 A.M. to dusk. The Fox Nature Center is open Memorial Day weekend to Labor Day, Monday through Friday, from 8:00 A.M. to 4:00 P.M.; and on Saturday, Sunday, and holidays, from 10:00 A.M. to 4:00 P.M.

ENTRANCE FEE: None.

HANDICAP ACCESS: The Nature Center, the boardwalk trail, the picnic area, and restrooms are handicap accessible.

SPECIAL FEATURES

Fox Nature Center—Displays depicting some of the area's history, and plant and animal life. There are live animal displays and information. For more information, call (609) 625-1897.

CAMPING: Eight family tent sites, with fire rings and tables, restrooms, and drinking water.

PICNICKING: Tables with grills, with a playground and a restroom.

BOATING: Access to the South River (boat launch for trailer boats), and Stevens Creek (hand-carried boats only).

FISHING: Permitted in the South River and in Stevens Creek, for white and yellow perch, pickerel, and catfish.

HIKING: More than thirteen miles of marked trails.

MOUNTAIN BIKING: Permitted on designated trails.

HORSEBACK RIDING: Permitted on designated trails.

BIRDWATCHING: Observation booths for birdwatching.

HUNTING: For deer and waterfowl, with a county permit.

WINTER ACTIVITIES: Cross-country skiing.

For additional information:
Atlantic County Parks System
109 State Highway 50
Mays Landing, NJ 08330
Telephone: (609) 625-1897

For permits and reservations:
Atlantic County Parks System
6303 Old Harding Highway
Mays Landing, NJ 08330
Telephone: (609) 625-8219

Fortescue Wildlife Management Area

Fortescue Road • Fortescue, Cumberland County •
1,161 acres

LOCATION: Access is from Fortescue Road, between Newport and Fortescue, on the Delaware Bay.

HOURS: Dawn to dusk.

ENTRANCE FEE: None.

FISHING: Permitted in tidal creeks, for white perch, and also in the Delaware Bay.

CRABBING: Permitted in tidal creeks and in the bay.

HUNTING: For small game and waterfowl.

For additional information:
New Jersey Division of Fish and Wildlife
Trenton Office
501 E. State Street, P.O. Box 400
Trenton, NJ 08625–0400
Telephone: (609) 984-0547

 Gaskill Park

River Road • Mays Landing, Atlantic County • 10 acres

LOCATION: Located at the head of the Egg Harbor River in Mays Landing, adjacent to the Atlantic County Library.

HOURS: Dawn to dusk.

ENTRANCE FEE: None.

HANDICAP ACCESS: The bulkhead for fishing, the floating docks, the picnic area, and restrooms are handicap accessible.

FISHING: Permitted in the Egg Harbor River. Bulkhead and floating docks available.

PICNICKING: Tables and grills, with a playground and restrooms.

For additional information:
Atlantic County Parks System
109 State Highway 50
Mays Landing, NJ 08330
Telephone: (609) 625-1897

For permits and reservations:
Atlantic County Parks System
6303 Old Harding Highway
Mays Landing, NJ 08330
Telephone: (609) 625-8219

Gibson Creek
Wildlife Management Area

Atlantic County ◆ *1,203 acres*

LOCATION: Adjacent to Route 557, and west of the town of Oakville.

HOURS: Dawn to dusk.

ENTRANCE FEE: None.

HANDICAP ACCESS: None.

HIKING: Informal trails.

MOUNTAIN BIKING: Allowed on existing trails and secondary roads from March 1 to April 15, and from June 1 to September 15, as well as on all Sundays throughout the year.

HUNTING: For deer, small game, turkey, and waterfowl.

WINTER ACTIVITIES: Cross-country skiing on all trails on Sunday.

For additional information:
New Jersey Division of Fish and Wildlife
Trenton Office
501 E. State Street, P.O. Box 400
Trenton, NJ 08625-0400
Telephone: (609) 984-0547

Gum Tree Corner
Wildlife Management Area

Cumberland County ◆ *791 acres*

LOCATION: Located west of Route 49, near the town of Gum Tree Corner.

HOURS: Dawn to dusk.

ENTRANCE FEE: None.

HANDICAP ACCESS: None.

BOATING: Allowed in Stow Creek.

FISHING: Permitted in Stow Creek.

CRABBING: Permitted in Stow Creek.

HIKING: Informal trails.

MOUNTAIN BIKING: Allowed on existing trails and secondary roads from March 1 to April 15, and from June 1 to September 15, as well as on all Sundays throughout the year.

HUNTING: For deer, small game, turkey, and waterfowl.

WINTER ACTIVITIES: Cross-country skiing on all trails on Sunday.

> **For additional information:**
> *New Jersey Division of Fish and Wildlife*
> *Trenton Office*
> *501 E. State Street, P.O. Box 400*
> *Trenton, NJ 08625—0400*
> *Telephone: (609) 984-0547*

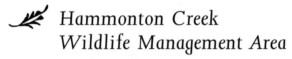

Hammonton Creek
Wildlife Management Area

Atlantic County • *1,757 acres*

LOCATION: Located south of Route 542, and east of Route 561.

HOURS: Dawn to dusk.

ENTRANCE FEE: None.

HANDICAP ACCESS: None.

HIKING: Informal trails.

MOUNTAIN BIKING: Allowed on existing trails and secondary roads from March 1 to April 15, and from June 1 to September 15, as well as on all Sundays throughout the year.

HUNTING: For deer, small game, and turkey.

WINTER ACTIVITIES: Cross-country skiing on all trails on Sunday.

> **For additional information:**
> *New Jersey Division of Fish and Wildlife*
> *Trenton Office*
> *501 E. State Street, P.O. Box 400*
> *Trenton, NJ 08625—0400*
> *Telephone: (609) 984-0547*

Hammonton Lake Park

Egg Harbor Road and Park Avenue ✦ *Hammonton,*
Atlantic County ✦ *10 acres*

LOCATION: Located south of Route 542, and west of Route 30.

HOURS: The grounds are open from 7:00 A.M. to dusk. The swimming area is open Memorial Day weekend to Labor Day, Tuesday through Sunday, from 12:00 P.M. to 6:00 P.M. Call to confirm opening.

ENTRANCE FEE: None.

HANDICAP ACCESS: Swimming and picnic areas are flat and easily accessible.

BOATING: Allowed in 75-acre Hammonton Lake. Boat ramp available for trailer and car-top boats. No gas motors.

SWIMMING: Swimming can be enjoyed in the lake. Restrooms are open during the swimming season only. For more information, call the lifeguard station: (609) 567-4355.

FISHING: Permitted in the lake.

PICNICKING: Tables, some with grills, a playground, and restrooms near the swimming area.

> **For additional information:**
> Hammonton Recreation Department
> 100 Central Avenue
> Hammonton, NJ 08037
> Telephone: (609) 567-4341

 # Heislerville Wildlife Management Area

Matts Landing, East Point, and Thompson Beach Roads ✦
Cumberland County ✦ *6,291 acres*

LOCATION: Across from Route 47, and southwest of Delmont, on the Delaware Bay.

HOURS: Dawn to dusk.

ENTRANCE FEE: None.

HANDICAP ACCESS: None.

FISHING: Permitted in the Maurice River, in the surrounding tidal creeks, and in the Delaware Bay.

HUNTING: For deer, small game, and waterfowl.

Note: Thompsons Beach and Moores Beach are the site of horse-shoe crab spawning, and the principal feeding grounds for red knots, ruddy turnstones, dunlin, and semipalmated sandpipers during May of each year.

For additional information:
New Jersey Division of Fish and Wildlife
Trenton Office
501 E. State Street, P.O. Box 400
Trenton, NJ 08625–0400
Telephone: (609) 984-0547

Higbee Beach
Wildlife Management Area

New England Road • Cap May County • 1,033 acres

LOCATION: The parking area is at the end of New England Road, west of Route 607 (Bay Shore Road). From there, a dirt road leads to the jetty.

HOURS: Dawn to dusk.

Greg Johnson

Higbee Beach Wildlife Management Area.

ENTRANCE FEE: None.

HANDICAP ACCESS: None.

DESCRIPTION: Known for its exceptional birding, Higbee Beach is also the place to find "Cape May diamonds"—semiprecious quartz pebbles that resemble diamonds.

FISHING: Permitted in 4.5-acre Daveys Lake, for freshwater fish. There is surf fishing in the Delaware Bay. A jetty on the north end of the beach provides additional fishing opportunities.

HIKING: Informal trails.

MOUNTAIN BIKING: Allowed on existing trails and secondary roads from March 1 to April 15, and from June 1 to September 15, as well as on all Sundays throughout the year.

HORSEBACK RIDING: Allowed on all trails, with a permit.

BIRDWATCHING: There is an observation tower.

HUNTING: For small game and waterfowl.

WINTER ACTIVITIES: Cross-country skiing on all trails on Sunday.

Note: Regulations affecting use in the fall vary from other Wildlife Management areas. Call for more specific information.

For additional information:
New Jersey Division of Fish and Wildlife
Trenton Office
501 E. State Street, P.O. Box 400
Trenton, NJ 08625–0400
Telephone: (609) 984-0547

 Lenape Park

Mays Landing, Atlantic County   •   1,900 acres

LOCATION: Located south of Route 322, and west of Route 50, on the southeast shore of Lake Lenape.

HOURS: The grounds are open from dawn to dusk. The boathouse/reservations office is open daily, Memorial Day through Labor Day, from 7:30 A.M. to 10:00 P.M., and off-season, daily, from 7:30 A.M. to 5:00 P.M.

ENTRANCE FEE: None.

HANDICAP ACCESS: The boathouse area, the floating dock, and the restrooms/showers are handicap accessible.

CAMPING: Eighteen family tent sites, with tables and fire rings, pit toilets, and drinking water. Portable toilets are located in the camping area; restrooms and showers are a short walk away in the boathouse area.

BOATING: Allowed in 344-acre Lake Lenape. A boat launch is available for trailer and car-top boats. Boats with motors in excess of 9.9 horsepower require a permit.

FISHING: Permitted in the lake, which is stocked with bass.

HIKING: Approximately ten miles of marked trails, including one self-guided trail with brochure.

HUNTING: For deer and waterfowl, with a county permit.

WINTER ACTIVITIES: Cross-country skiing.

For additional information:
Atlantic County Parks System
109 State Highway 50
Mays Landing, NJ 08330
Telephone: (609) 625-1897

For permits and reservations:
Atlantic County Parks System
6303 Old Harding Highway
Mays Landing, NJ 08330
Telephone: (609) 625-8219

Makepeace Lake
Wildlife Management Area

Elwood-Weymouth Road ♦ Hamilton and Mullica
Townships ♦ Atlantic County ♦ 10,145 acres

LOCATION: Located between Route 322 (Black Horse Pike) and Route 30 (White Horse Pike), in Hamilton and Mullica Townships. Access to the tract is from Elwood-Weymouth Road, near Egg Harbor City. The Atlantic City Expressway bisects the tract.

HOURS: Dawn to dusk.

ENTRANCE FEE: None.

HANDICAP ACCESS: None.

BOATING: A car-top boat launch is available on Elwood-Weymouth Road.

FISHING: Permitted in 300-acre Makepeace Lake. The lake is very shallow, with an average depth of three to four feet. Fish are limited to pickerel and catfish.

HUNTING: For small game and waterfowl, and trapping for beaver and otter.

For additional information:
New Jersey Division of Fish and Wildlife
Trenton Office
501 E. State Street, P.O. Box 400
Trenton, NJ 08625–0400
Telephone: (609) 984-0547

 # Maple Lake Wildlife Management Area

Atlantic County ◆ 460 acres

LOCATION: Located east of Route 557, near the town of Estellville.

HOURS: Dawn to dusk.

ENTRANCE FEE: None.

HANDICAP ACCESS: None.

BOATING: Allowed in 35-acre Maple Lake. A boat ramp and car-top boat launch are available.

FISHING: Permitted in the lake, for pickerel, yellow perch, and largemouth bass.

HIKING: Informal trails.

MOUNTAIN BIKING: Allowed on existing trails and secondary roads from March 1 to April 15, and from June 1 to September 15, as well as on all Sundays throughout the year.

HUNTING: For deer, small game, turkey, and waterfowl.

WINTER ACTIVITIES: Cross-country skiing on all trails on Sunday.

For additional information:
New Jersey Division of Fish and Wildlife
Trenton Office
501 E. State Street, P.O. Box 400
Trenton, NJ 08625–0400
Telephone: (609) 984-0547

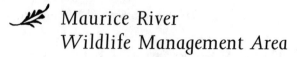

Maurice River
Wildlife Management Area

Cumberland County ◆ 269 acres

LOCATION: Located west of Route 55, exit 21.

HOURS: Dawn to dusk.

ENTRANCE FEE: None.

HANDICAP ACCESS: None.

BOATING: Allowed in the Maurice River.

FISHING: Permitted in the river.

HUNTING: For waterfowl.

> **For additional information:**
> New Jersey Division of Fish and Wildlife
> Trenton Office
> 501 E. State Street, P.O. Box 400
> Trenton, NJ 08625–0400
> Telephone: (609) 984-0547

Menantico Ponds
Wildlife Management Area

Route 49 ◆ Cumberland County ◆ 394 acres

LOCATION: The access road is off Route 49, east of Millville, and just east of the Menantico Creek crossing, heading south.

HOURS: Dawn to dusk.

ENTRANCE FEE: None.

HANDICAP ACCESS: None.

BOATING: Car-top boats and electric motors only. A boat ramp is located at the end of the access road.

FISHING: Permitted in the 62-acre ponds.

HIKING: Informal trails.

MOUNTAIN BIKING: Allowed on existing trails and secondary roads from March 1 to April 15, and from June 1 to September 15, as well as on all Sundays throughout the year.

HUNTING: For deer, small game, turkey, and waterfowl.

WINTER ACTIVITIES: Cross-country skiing on all trails on Sunday.

For additional information:
New Jersey Division of Fish and Wildlife
Trenton Office
501 E. State Street, P.O. Box 400
Trenton, NJ 08625–0400
Telephone: (609) 984-0547

Millville Wildlife Management Area

Route 555 ♦ Cumberland County ♦ 12,838 acres

LOCATION: North of Route 553 and the town of Dividing Creek. Route 555 bisects the tract.

HOURS: Dawn to dusk.

ENTRANCE FEE: None.

HANDICAP ACCESS: None.

BOATING: Allowed in Shaw's Mill Pond (30 acres), with car-top boat launch.

FISHING: Permitted at Shaw's Mill Pond, located off Route 629 (Newport-Center Grove Road), in the southwest corner of the tract. The pond is stocked with trout, and there is excellent fishing for largemouth bass.

HIKING: Informal trails.

MOUNTAIN BIKING: Allowed on existing trails and secondary roads from March 1 to April 15, and from June 1 to September 15, as well as on all Sundays throughout the year.

HORSEBACK RIDING: Allowed on trails, with a permit.

HUNTING: For deer, small game, turkey, and waterfowl.

WINTER ACTIVITIES: Cross-country skiing on all trails on Sunday.

For additional information:
New Jersey Division of Fish and Wildlife
Trenton Office
501 E. State Street, P.O. Box 400
Trenton, NJ 08625–0400
Telephone: (609) 984-0547

Nantuxent Wildlife Management Area

Cumberland County ◆ *1,340 acres*

LOCATION: South of Cedarville. Access is from Bay Point Road.

HOURS: Dawn to dusk.

ENTRANCE FEE: None.

HANDICAP ACCESS: None.

BOATING: Allowed in 57-acre Cedar Lake.

FISHING: Permitted in Nantuxent Creek and in Cedar Lake.

HUNTING: For deer, small game, turkey, and waterfowl.

> **For additional information:**
> New Jersey Division of Fish and Wildlife
> Trenton Office
> 501 E. State Street, P.O. Box 400
> Trenton, NJ 08625–0400
> Telephone: (609) 984-0547

New Sweden Wildlife Management Area

Cumberland County ◆ *2,238 acres*

LOCATION: West of Route 553. Access is from Bay Point Road (Route 610).

HOURS: Dawn to dusk.

ENTRANCE FEE: None.

HANDICAP ACCESS: None.

BOATING: Allowed in the Delaware Bay and in the Cohansey River.

FISHING: Permitted in the Delaware Bay and in the Cohansey River.

CRABBING: Permitted in the Delaware Bay.

HUNTING: For waterfowl.

> **For additional information:**
> New Jersey Division of Fish and Wildlife
> Trenton Office
> 501 E. State Street, P.O. Box 400
> Trenton, NJ 08625–0400
> Telephone: (609) 984-0547

Peaslee Wildlife Management Area

Route 49 • Cumberland and Cape May Counties •
25,572 acres

LOCATION: Approximately 7 miles east of Millville. Route 49 offers access to a large portion of the tract.

HOURS: Dawn to dusk.

ENTRANCE FEE: None.

HANDICAP ACCESS: None.

BOATING: A car-top launch is available for the Tuckahoe River.

FISHING: Permitted in the river.

HIKING: Informal trails.

MOUNTAIN BIKING: Allowed on existing trails and secondary roads from March 1 to April 15, and from June 1 to September 15, as well as on all Sundays throughout the year.

HORSEBACK RIDING: Allowed on trails, with a permit.

HUNTING: For deer, small game, wild turkey, and waterfowl.

WINTER ACTIVITIES: Cross-country skiing on all trails on Sunday.

> **For additional information:**
> New Jersey Division of Fish and Wildlife
> Trenton Office
> 501 E. State Street, P.O. Box 400
> Trenton, NJ 08625–0400
> Telephone: (609) 984-0547

Pork Island Wildlife Management Area

Atlantic County • 831 acres

LOCATION: Bisected by Route 563, and northwest of Margate.

HOURS: Dawn to dusk.

ENTRANCE FEE: None.

HANDICAP ACCESS: None.

BOATING: Allowed in the bay.

FISHING: Permitted in the bay.

CRABBING: Permitted in the bay.

HUNTING: For waterfowl.

> **For additional information:**
> *New Jersey Division of Fish and Wildlife*
> *Trenton Office*
> *501 E. State Street, P.O. Box 400*
> *Trenton, NJ 08625–0400*
> *Telephone: (609) 984-0547*

 # Port Republic Wildlife Management Area

Atlantic County ◆ *1,347 acres*

LOCATION: North of Port Republic. The tract is bordered on the east by the Garden State Parkway, and on the north by the Mullica River. Access to the tract is from Clarks Landing Road, to an unpaved road leading northeast, parallel to the Garden State Parkway.

HOURS: Dawn to dusk.

ENTRANCE FEE: None.

HANDICAP ACCESS: None.

BOATING: Launching ramps and boat rentals are available in the surrounding area.

FISHING: Saltwater fishing in the Mullica River, which borders the tract. Striped bass and white perch are the primary species.

CRABBING: Permitted.

HUNTING: For deer, small game, and waterfowl.

WINTER ACTIVITIES: Ice fishing for white perch in Collins Cove.

> **For additional information:**
> *New Jersey Division of Fish and Wildlife*
> *Trenton Office*
> *501 E. State Street, P.O. Box 400*
> *Trenton, NJ 08625–0400*
> *Telephone: (609) 984-0547*

 # River Bend

Egg Harbor Township, Atlantic County ◆ *774 acres*

LOCATION: West of Route 559, along the Great Egg Harbor River.

HOURS: Dawn to dusk.

ENTRANCE FEE: None.

HANDICAP ACCESS: Restrooms (located at the public shooting range) are handicap accessible. Restrooms are open year-round and daily, when the range is open, from 8:00 A.M. to 4:00 P.M., as well as some nights.

FISHING: Permitted in the Great Egg Harbor River.

HIKING: Informal hiking trails.

MOUNTAIN BIKING: Permitted on trails.

HORSEBACK RIDING: Permitted on trails.

HUNTING: For deer and waterfowl, with a county permit.

WINTER ACTIVITIES: Cross-country skiing.

Note: Visitors to the park during the winter, while hunting season is in progress, are advised to wear blaze orange.

For additional information:
Atlantic County Parks System
109 State Highway 50
Mays Landing, NJ 08330
Telephone: (609) 625-1897

For permits and reservations:
Atlantic County Parks System
6303 Old Harding Highway
Mays Landing, NJ 08330
Telephone: (609) 625-8219

 ## Tuckahoe Wildlife Management Area

Route 50 ◆ *Atlantic and Cape May Counties* ◆
14,127 acres

LOCATION: East of Tuckahoe, on Route 50. The office is located on Tuckahoe-Marmara Road, north of Petersburg.

HOURS: Dawn to dusk.

ENTRANCE FEE: None.

HANDICAP ACCESS: None.

BOATING: A boat ramp is located east of Tuckahoe, providing access to Great Egg Harbor River and Bay.

FISHING: Six lakes are located in the tract.

HUNTING: For deer, small game, and waterfowl; trapping for muskrats and mink.

For additional information:
New Jersey Division of Fish and Wildlife
Trenton Office
501 E. State Street, P.O. Box 400
Trenton, NJ 08625–0400
Telephone: (609) 984-0547

 # Union Lake Wildlife Management Area

Route 55 ◆ Cumberland and Salem Counties ◆
4,965 acres

LOCATION: Just northwest of Millville, and west of Route 55.

HOURS: Dawn to dusk.

ENTRANCE FEE: None.

HANDICAP ACCESS: None.

DESCRIPTION: Includes the largest lake in southern New Jersey, at 898 acres and a maximum depth of nearly thirty feet.

BOATING: Allowed in the 898-acre lake. A boat ramp is available for trailer and car-top access.

FISHING: Excellent fishing, primarily for largemouth bass, striped bass, chain pickerel, white and yellow perch, and channel catfish.

HIKING: Informal trails.

HORSEBACK RIDING: Permitted on trails.

MOUNTAIN BIKING: Allowed on existing trails and secondary roads from March 1 to April 15, and from June 1 to September 15, as well as on all Sundays throughout the year.

HUNTING: For deer, small game, turkey, and waterfowl.

WINTER ACTIVITIES: Cross-country skiing on all trails on Sunday.

For additional information:
New Jersey Division of Fish and Wildlife
Trenton Office
501 E. State Street, P.O. Box 400
Trenton, NJ 08625–0400
Telephone: (609) 984-0547

The Wetlands Institute

Stone Harbor Boulevard ♦ *Stone Harbor* ♦ *34 acres*

LOCATION: Just east of the Garden State Parkway, exit 10, on Stone Harbor Boulevard.

HOURS: Open May 15 to October 15, Monday through Saturday, from 9:30 A.M. to 4:30 P.M.; and from October 16 through May 14, Tuesday to Saturday, from 9:30 A.M. to 4:30 P.M.

ENTRANCE FEE: None.

HANDICAP ACCESS: The main building is handicap accessible.

DESCRIPTION: A private, nonprofit organization dedicated to research and public education concerning wetlands and coastal ecosystems.

HIKING: A trail and boardwalk traverse the salt marsh. Self-guided year-round, and guided in the summer.

For additional information:
1075 Stone Harbor Boulevard
Stone Harbor, NJ 08247–1424
Telephone: (609) 368-1211

 # Weymouth County Park

Hamilton Township, Atlantic County ♦ *6 acres*

LOCATION: At the intersection of Route 322 and Route 559, just north of the Black Horse Pike.

HOURS: Dawn to dusk.

ENTRANCE FEE: None.

HANDICAP ACCESS: None.

DESCRIPTION: The site of the foundation of Weymouth Iron Forge and Papermill.

BOATING: Canoe access to the Great Egg Harbor River.

FISHING: Permitted in the river.

PICNICKING: Tables with grills, and portable toilet.

For additional information:
Atlantic County Parks System
109 State Highway 50
Mays Landing, NJ 08330
Telephone: (609) 625-1897

For permits and reservations:
Atlantic County Parks System
6303 Old Harding Highway
Mays Landing, NJ 08330
Telephone: (609) 625-8219

 # Whirlpool Island County Park

Shelter Island Bay ◆ Northfield ◆ *185 acres*

LOCATION: South of the Atlantic City Expressway, and east of Route 9.

HOURS: Dawn to dusk.

ENTRANCE FEE: None.

HANDICAP ACCESS: None.

FISHING: Permitted in the Shelter Island Bay. (Accessible only by boat.)

HUNTING: For waterfowl, with a county permit.

For additional information:
Atlantic County Parks System
109 State Highway 50
Mays Landing, NJ 08330
Telephone: (609) 625-1897

For permits and reservations:
Atlantic County Parks System
6303 Old Harding Highway
Mays Landing, NJ 08330
Telephone: (609) 625-8219

Bibliography

General

Burger, Joanna, and Michael Gochfeld. *Twenty-Five Nature Spectacles in New Jersey.* Piscataway, N.J.: Rutgers University Press, 2000.

Rosenfeld, Lucy D., and Marina Harrison. *A Guide to Green New Jersey: Nature Walks in the Garden State.* Piscataway, N.J.: Rutgers University Press, 2003.

Zatz, Arline. *New Jersey's Great Gardens: A Four-Season Guide to 125 Public Gardens, Parks, and Arboretums.* Woodstock, Vt.: Countryman Press, 2003.

Birdwatching

Boyle, William J., Jr. *A Guide to Bird Finding in New Jersey.* Piscataway, N.J.: Rutgers University Press, 2002.

Boating

Cawley, James, and Margaret Cawley. *Exploring the Little Rivers of New Jersey.* 4th ed. Piscataway, N.J.: Rutgers University Press, 1993.

Kenley, Kathy. *Quiet Water New Jersey: Canoe & Kayak Guide.* Boston: Appalachian Mountain Club Books, 2001.

Parnes, Robert. *Paddling the Jersey Pine Barrens.* 6th ed. Guilford, Conn.: Falcon, 2002.

Fishing

Freda, Jim. *Fishing the New Jersey Coast.* Short Hills, N.J.: Burford Books, 2001.

Hiking

Della Penna, Craig P. *24 Great Rail-Trails of New Jersey*. Amherst, Mass.: New England Cartographics, 1999.

Scofield, Bruce C., Stella Green, and H. Neil Zimmerman. *50 Hikes in New Jersey: Hikes, Walks, and Backpacking Trips from the Kittatinnys to Cape May*. 2nd ed. Woodstock, Vt.: Backcountry Publications, 2003.

Mountain Biking

MacKinnan, Christopher. *Mountain Biking in New Jersey: 45 Off-Road Rides in the Garden State*. Lahaska, Pa.: Freewheeling Press, 2003.

Index